She
PRAYS

A 31-DAY JOURNEY
TO CONFIDENT
CONVERSATIONS
WITH GOD

DEBBIE LINDELL

Revell
a division of Baker Publishing Group
Grand Rapids, Michigan

Published by Revell
a division of Baker Publishing Group
PO Box 6287, Grand Rapids, MI 49516-6287
www.revellbooks.com

Printed in the United States of America

Library of Congress Cataloging-in-Publication Data
Names: Lindell, Debbie, author.
Title: She prays : a 31-day journey to confident conversations with God / Debbie Lindell.
Description: Grand Rapids, MI : Revell, a division of Baker Publishing Group, [2019]
Identifiers: LCCN 2019011776 I ISBN 9780800736828 (pbk.)
Subjects: LCSH: Christian women—Prayers and devotions. I Christian women—Religious life.
Classification: LCC BV4844 .L56 2019 I DDC 242/.643—dc23
LC record available at https://lccn.loc.gov/2019011776

Photos by Meshali.

20 21 22 23 24 25   7 6 5 4 3 2

To my grandma Alice
and my mom, Bonnie—
your faith-filled prayers for me
are the thread that wove
these words together.

Contents

Contents

Foreword

Several years ago, not long after I'd brought my adopted daughter Missy home from Haiti, we had a precious conversation that changed the topography of my theology regarding prayer. We were lying on a bed together one warm summer afternoon with wildly divergent goals: Missy, who was five years old at the time, was diligently trying to dodge a nap, while I was desperately trying to get her to take one. She employed what has since become a very effective nap- and chore-dodging strategy: she began asking questions about God because she knows that's my hot button.

Here's our conversation as best I remember it:

> **Missy:** Mommy, what do you think God and Jebus are doing in heaven right now?
>
> **Me:** Well, honey, what do *you* think God and Jesus are doing in heaven right now? (I responded in

this Socratic manner because several dear friends who had much more parenting experience than I did told me that when your toddler asks a complex question, it's a good idea to pose it back to them!)

Missy: I think they're talking about me!

Me: That's probably true, baby, because the Bible says that Jesus sits at the right hand of God the Father and intercedes on our behalf, which means they do talk to each other about us.

Missy: What do you think God and Jebus are saying about me, Mommy?

Me: Hmmm, what do *you* think they're saying about you, toots?

Missy (pauses for about thirty seconds before her face splits into a grin): I think Jebus just pointed down at me and said, "*I lub that Missy!*"

In that moment I realized my little girl—who had been orphaned as a baby when her first mama died of un-diagnosed AIDS, left starving for both physical and emotional nourishment in a rural third world village afterward, and then given a slim chance of surviving by medical professionals in Port-au-Prince—was actually thriving. And not just physically and emotionally; she was truly thriving in her relationship with God! Plus her understanding of our Lord's affectionate predisposition toward his image bearers was more theologically sound and biblically defensible than mine.

This is why I so appreciate the message of my dear friend Debbie Lindell's newest literary project, *She Prays*. This is not a perky self-help tome for sissy supplicants, y'all. Nor is it a guilt-inducing, humble-brag fest written by some self-appointed saint who gets up at 3:00 a.m. and sequesters herself in a custom prayer closet for hours on end, after which she journals about it in her all-white chef-appointed kitchen while the delicious scents of casseroles she's baking for the needy waft from her shiny, stainless, double convection ovens (not that I'm remotely bitter about spiritual overachievers or anything). Nope, this book is for real women—you know, the ones with French fries littering the floorboards of their minivans, with coffee stains on their Bible studies, and whose kids or grandkids usually have sticky hands and missing homework. These women desperately need to be reminded that they have the full attention and unconditional affection of a real God who actually enjoys hearing from them!

Frankly, I think far too many believers view prayer as an obligatory exercise of spiritual duty and discipline instead of the joy- and awe-filled overflow of a real relationship with God. And to be fair, many of us have been taught the former by well-meaning preachers, teachers, and pundits. Take, for instance, what some refer to as the "how to pray" parable in Luke's Gospel:

And he said to them, "Which of you who has a friend will go to him at midnight and say to him, 'Friend, lend me three loaves, for a friend of mine has arrived on a journey, and I have nothing to set before him'; and he will answer from within, 'Do not bother me; the door is now shut, and my children are with me in bed. I cannot get up and give you anything'? I tell you, though he will not get up and give him anything because he is his friend, yet because of his impudence he will rise and give him whatever he needs. And I tell you, ask, and it will be given to you; seek, and you will find; knock, and it will be opened to you. For everyone who asks receives, and the one who seeks finds, and to the one who knocks it will be opened. What father among you, if his son asks for a fish, will instead of a fish give him a serpent; or if he asks for an egg, will give him a scorpion? If you then, who are evil, know how to give good gifts to your children, how much more will the heavenly Father give the Holy Spirit to those who ask him!"

Luke 11:5–13 ESV

I've often heard this passage explained so as to emphasize the need for diligence in prayer, and I completely agree that persistence in prayer is a good thing. In fact, one of my favorite quotes from John Calvin regarding prayer is, "We must repeat the same supplications not twice or three times only, but as often as we have a need, a hundred and a thousand times. . . . We must never weary in waiting for God's help."[1]

However, lest we reduce the joy of communing with our compassionate Creator-Redeemer to a dutiful exercise, I think it behooves us to keep in mind his sovereign benevolence toward us. God is not some supernatural sleepyhead who's reluctant to rouse himself and answer our cries for help, which is the problem with the common single-application interpretation of this parable. Jesus didn't share this story with the Twelve to imply they needed to twist Jehovah's arm to get him to act on their behalf. Rather, the rhetorical device he used (see also Luke 12:25) when he posed the question "How much more" puts the onus squarely on God. So the main point Jesus was driving home to those knuckleheads was much less about our tenacity in prayer and much more about the tenderness of our divine Dad.

Don't forget:

- He is the one who longs to give us good gifts (Matthew 7:11).
- He is the one who inclines his ear to hear us (Psalm 34:15).
- He is the one who initiates and sustains the relationship with us (Romans 5:8).

The bottom line is, this book isn't about God wagging his finger at us in disappointment over our sometimes anemic prayer life. It's about him pointing his finger at us in fatherly pride while declaring affectionately, "*I lub that one right there!"* I believe the touchstones regarding our Redeemer's compassion, which Debbie has beautifully woven throughout this book, are what will compel all of us to become she who prays!

Lisa Harper, author and Bible teacher

Introduction

I have been praying for you!

The fact that you are holding this book in your hands tells me God is working in your life. Wherever you are in your understanding of prayer, you have more to discover. And my hope and desire is for you to grow deeper in your knowledge of who God is, become more connected to his will, and be more intimately aware of his presence every moment of every day.

You might have picked up this book because you are walking through a difficult season and you very much want to feel closer to God. Maybe you have a longing in your heart to become more confident in your communication with your heavenly Father and you just aren't sure where to begin. Or possibly, like me, you want to know God more intimately and for your conversations with him to be full of faith and connected to his divine will and purpose.

Throughout my years in ministry, women at every level
of faith have expressed how they can feel intimidated
when it comes to talking to God. They say, "Debbie,
I don't know the words to pray" or "How do I know if
God hears me?" One girl recently opened up about
her feelings on social media and said, "I'm just terrible
at prayer." That comment broke my heart. Her words
revealed that she doesn't understand how excited her
heavenly Father is every time she opens up to him.
Somewhere in her past she began to feel pressure to act
and even talk a certain way. And because of her insecuri-
ties and lack of understanding, she is missing out on the
joy, the blessing, and the power found in relational, confident communication with her heavenly Father.

May I just tell you what prayer is not? It is not a religious
requirement or a measure of your faithfulness and commitment to God. It is not you saying things perfectly to
appease some disconnected deity who doesn't really
care to know you personally. It is not memorizing certain words and repeating them over and over. It is not
someone else more "qualified" than you talking and
connecting to God on your behalf. Prayer is coming to
understand the beauty and fullness of God's invitation
for you to draw near and talk with him personally about
everything, like a daughter would—fully trusting her
thoughts and emotions to a loving and caring earthly
father, without reservation or fear of rejection.

It's one thing to know that we're not gifted at public speaking, playing the violin, or making homemade pumpkin pie, but to believe that we are somehow unqualified or not gifted enough to communicate with our heavenly Father is quite honestly tragic. That's because prayer—in its pure form, apart from the pressures we attach to it—is our personal connection and lifeline to God.

But to be honest, I know exactly what it means to feel insecure when it comes to prayer. The truth is, prayer can be intimidating. To think that we are having a conversation with the most powerful being in the entire universe! The God who spoke all of creation into existence wants to listen to us and respond to us when we talk to him! That is an amazing and sometimes overwhelming thought. But it's true. We have an open invitation, anytime and anywhere, to talk to God. Through prayer, we draw close to God and he draws close to us. In prayer, he reveals his power, his character, his wisdom, his grace, and his amazing love for us. He invites us to partner alongside him in his redemptive work in the world.

No matter at what prayer level you would place yourself, I know God has more for you. His desire is for you to grow in your understanding and confidence regarding your conversations with him—to come to him more boldly and more confidently, believing that when you do, he is there to hear you and respond!

Throughout the next thirty-one days, my hope is to remove the pressures we attach to prayer, throw out the condemning lies we believe about it, and help you discover a faith marked by intimate, confident conversations with God. Each day you'll be invited to unfold the freeing truth about prayer and to open your heart to converse with him in a deeper, more intimate way than ever before.

I cannot tell you how excited I am for you! As you commit to this journey, I am confident that your prayer life will be transformed, that your faith will be strengthened, and that you'll see God move in and through your life in ways you never imagined!

SHE PRAYS
Understa

WITH
nding

PART ONE

An Open Door

Then as I looked, I saw a door standing open in heaven.

REVELATION 4:1

The door opened, and there she stood. Her face shone with joy as she welcomed my family in. The familiar scents of homemade *lefse* and sweet perfume brought me comfort. She was just over five feet tall, but she was a giant to my eight-year-old self. Her weathered Bible was lying open where it always was, on the little wooden table next to her worn floral chair with delicate crocheted doilies gracefully covering its arms. I always had the feeling that we had interrupted a conversation— one she was having with her best friend. And no doubt we were. She had loved and followed Jesus for over seventy-five years. She knew God. He was her heavenly Father, her friend, her protector, her counselor, her life, and her breath.

Her family had emigrated from Norway to northern Minnesota in 1882, a year before she was born. Life had not been easy for her: she had birthed ten children, lost one, and then sent four of her sons off to war. Her husband had struggled with severe depression, her sons had battled alcohol addiction, and her family endured the Great Depression. Yet through all the trials, her faith had become only stronger and her joy only more evident to all who knew her. How? She lived, breathed, and practiced God's presence, and because of that, his presence filled every part of her life. Her eyes sparkled with faith, hope, and trust. My little heart knew I wanted to be like her when I grew up. This tiny tower of a woman was my great-grandma Tina.

Everything moves. Nothing really stays the same. Grandmothers grow older, possessions become antiques, clocks tick, and time marches on. You? Well, you, my friend, are a little older since you began reading these words. You can't keep anything from changing.

Your prayer life is similar. It is either growing in strength or diminishing in power. If it's stagnant, like a pond without a fresh source of water flowing into it, it will gradually evaporate and become muddy. But God's presence and supernatural grace bring energy and vitality to your relationship with him like a stream flowing into your prayer life.

We live in a natural world. And if we are not careful to look through our spiritual eyes, it will be easy to think that the natural things are all there is to life. But the supernatural world exists. As a believer and follower of God, you have access to experience, touch, feel, and influence both the natural and spiritual realms.

Our day-to-day existence can seem completely void of the spiritual world. We get up, go to work, run errands, come home. We parent, converse with our spouses, manage our in-boxes, complete to-do lists. Even church can become routine—gray and empty and lifeless.

Pastor and author Simon Holley explains: "God is a supernatural being. He exists beyond and within the natural universe that he has created. This is part of what makes him God. He has created natural laws and prop-erties that control and regulate the universe that we live in. Part of our joy and delight is to study, understand and harness those laws for our benefit and advance-ment. However, the God who created those laws will not be contained by them. We see this throughout Scrip-ture. From the very first story of God walking with Adam in the cool of the day right through to the final stories of angelic battles in the book of Revelation, it is clear that

God's supernatural realm coexists with the natural realm that he has also created. The problem is we just don't see it."[1]

Our difficulty in being aware of the spiritual world isn't that it doesn't exist. The problem is that we don't step through the door of the natural world into all there is for us to experience in the supernatural world.

This past year I was at Disneyland with my family, and my daughter and I chose to visit an attraction together. We waited in a small room for several minutes, not knowing what was on the other side of a door. When the door opened, it revealed a large room with hundreds of seats. We sat down, and minutes later we seemed to be flying above the clouds, taking in spectacular color and brilliant scenery. It was magical and breathtaking, but to experience it, we first had to step through the door.

> **Your prayer life is the doorway to a place beyond your everyday, feet-on-the-ground life, into a whole new and colorful world.**

Your prayer life is the doorway to a place beyond your everyday, feet-on-the-ground life, into a whole new and colorful world. Prayer connects your natural world to the supernatural power and movement of your creator. You were granted access to this whole other world through your faith in Jesus Christ.

All this and more is what the apostle Paul was referring to in Ephesians 3:12 when he wrote, "Because of Christ and our faith in him, we can now come boldly and confidently into God's presence." You can go through the door! You have access to the supernatural, all-powerful Creator through prayer.

And just as Paul's desire was for believers to know and experience all that was beyond the door of the natural world, that is my desire for you. Through these next thirty-one days, I hope your prayer life will grow to another dimension; that your natural, everyday existence will tap into the color and vibrancy and power of the supernatural; and that you, my friend, will be changed forever.

Here is a paraphrase of Paul's writing in Ephesians 3:14 as I think about you and the exciting journey ahead:

> When I think of what God has made available to you, I go to my knees to pray to the Father, the Creator of everything, even your life. I pray that you will come to know and understand what is beyond the door of your natural, everyday life—to believe that through your daily encounters with your creator through prayer, you will be made complete, connecting fully and confidently to the supernatural power available to you in God's presence.

One time when Jesus was teaching, he said these words to everyone listening: "Ask, and you will receive; seek, and you will find; knock, and the door will be opened to you" (Matthew 7:7 GNT). What do you think those words might mean for your prayer life?

Imagine a door in front of you. God is about to open it and invite you inside to experience a deeper relationship with him. How does that make you feel? What would be the first thing you would want to ask him to do for you?

It Starts Here

I am the door. If anyone enters by me, he will be saved.

JOHN 10:9 ESV

On a Sunday morning a few years ago, a girl walked through the door of our church. This was her first time to walk into a church other than the one she had been raised in, the one where she had attended weekly Mass. All she knew about God was what she had seen and heard about him growing up. And all she knew about prayer was that it was a necessary requirement to be a "good" person.

She never looked forward to or took joy in talking to God. Her view was that talking to him was what she had to do to get rid of her sin, and her prayers were connected to embarrassment, shame, and humiliation. Her experience was confessing to a priest everything bad she had done so he could tell her what "prayers" to repeat to be absolved of her sinfulness. All this felt empty and meaningless, and her feelings of guilt and condemnation never seemed to go away. She didn't understand why, but she thought that was just the way it had to be.

Until that day.

When she walked into our church, what she saw immediately intrigued and amazed her. There was something different about this church. The people were talking with one another, obviously happy and excited to be there. During the service, her heart raced as she listened to the message. For the first time in her life she heard about a loving God who sent his Son, Jesus, so she could have a personal relationship with him. She thought, *This is incredible. I've finally found a place where I can hear the truth about Jesus!*

A few weeks later she made the decision to follow Jesus, accepted his forgiveness, and put her faith in him forever. That changed everything!

———

At the center of a vibrant relationship with God is a vibrant prayer life. And a vibrant prayer life begins and flourishes from one place—the forgiveness and grace of Jesus Christ. Because of sin, we were locked out of God's presence. Sin created a barrier between humanity and the divine, between our brokenness and his perfection, an impenetrable wall between us and God.

> At the center of a vibrant relationship with God is a vibrant prayer life.

We could do nothing to measure up—ever. On our own, we could never scale the wall to get to God.

But the best news you will ever hear is this: because of *his great love for us*, God provided a door for you and me to enter so we could come close to him and talk with him openly, freely, and confidently. That door is his Son, Jesus.

Jesus put it this way in John 14:6: "I am the way, and the truth, and the life. No one comes to the Father except through me" (ESV). Jesus took our sin upon himself, taking our place on the cross so that when we believe in him we can receive the love of God. His sacrifice opened the door that had been dead bolted by our sin—he broke the lock! And when he did, the door swung open wide, making it possible for us to run freely into the presence of God.

Jesus makes the connection possible. Without him, we'd have no way to communicate with God, no solution to our separation. But because of Jesus, we can pass through the door God made for us and draw near to the throne of grace. As the letter to the Hebrews tells us, we can now boldly, with complete assurance, enter heaven's "Most Holy Place because of the blood of Jesus. By his death, Jesus opened a new and life-giving way" into the throne room (Hebrews 10:19–20).

The most important thing you will ever hear about prayer is this: it begins with Jesus. He is the starting point. If you desire to draw closer to God, you must look into the face of his Son. Otherwise, you will forever strive to have a personal relationship with God without understanding how.

Not long ago, this same sweet girl told me, "Before I found Jesus, when I tried to pray, I felt like I needed to do everything right. . . . Now I can go to God with whatever is in my heart and I know that he is there to hear me. Jesus made the way for me to have my very own personal relationship with him!"

> **If you desire to draw closer to God, you must look into the face of his Son.**

I love how Charles Spurgeon sums up what happens when a heart awakens to the glorious truth of Jesus: "For a soul to come to Jesus is the grandest event in its history. It is spiritually dead till that day, but then it begins to live."[1]

It's as if when you accept Jesus, your soul is awakened to all that God intended for you to experience in him— freedom from sin *and* much, much more. It's as if he unlocks the door to his presence, opens it wide, and says, "Come inside, my dear one. I want you to get to know everything about me and to feel completely comfortable in my presence so I can make your life full and complete."

In John 10:7, Jesus said, "Truly, truly, I say to you, I am the door" (ESV). The more you seek Jesus, the more he'll reveal the Father's heart to you. It all starts with Jesus. But it's up to you to accept this new and glorious invitation for a relationship with your creator and heavenly Father. This invitation to believe and follow Jesus goes out to every single girl, no matter where she has been, what she has done, or what she has been taught to believe. The door is there for her to walk through. How amazing is that?

Take time to reflect on how Jesus made a way to God for you. Then either write out a prayer in your own words or pray the prayer below, thanking God for sending his Son, Jesus, to open the door for you to know him personally.

Heavenly Father, I am in awe of all you did to make it possible for me to experience the fullness of your amazing love and grace. Thank you for sending your Son, Jesus, to make a way for me to know you personally. Help me to grow in my understanding of what access into your presence means for me every day. Amen.

A Curtain Torn

He opened for us a new way, a living way, through the curtain.

HEBREWS 10:20 GNT

Before Jesus, people had only one way to approach God—a careful process that involved traveling to the temple, cleansing themselves, and presenting sacrificial offerings. And there in the temple, the separation between God's holiness and fallen humanity was visually represented by a wall-to-wall, floor-to-ceiling curtain.

The curtain was ornate, woven with blue, scarlet, and purple thread and displaying images of angels. This art piece was considered a marvel by historians like Josephus. Though beautiful, the curtain was functional, too, and it hung as a barrier between the holy of holies, a room where God's presence hovered over the ark of the covenant, and the worshippers in the sanctuary.

Because of sin, no one could physically, emotionally, or spiritually connect with God, and the curtain served as a reminder of that reality. The sin and brokenness were so great that no number of sacrifices or offerings, no amount of cleansing, could make a person holy and pure enough to meet personally with God. But then Jesus came, and everything changed. He took our place on the cross, giving the ultimate sacrifice of his own life. Look at Mark 15:37–38: "Then Jesus uttered another loud cry and breathed his last. And the curtain in the sanctuary of the Temple was torn in two, from top to bottom." The curtain of separation was gone forever.

Jesus bore our punishment. He took our place and rectified our debt. There was no longer a need for offerings or sacrifices—only for surrendered hearts. There was no longer a need for the curtain to separate the sinners and the sinless—only intimate communion with our creator. Jesus's sacrifice made it possible for us to pray anytime, anywhere. This is one of the most beautiful gifts of salvation—how accessible God has made himself to us through prayer.

> **Jesus's sacrifice made it possible for us to pray anytime, anywhere.**

Through faith in Christ, we remember that God made a way for us to draw near to him no matter what. From the beginning, he's always been the one who initiates intimacy. He loves us so much that he did everything necessary to break through the obstacles of sinful humanity just to be with us.

God tore down the curtain. He made the move; we simply respond. And now you and I can trust that even when it feels like he's far away, he's closer than we could ever dream. Philippians 4:5–6 says, "The Lord is near. Do not be anxious about anything, but in every situation, by prayer and petition, with thanksgiving, present your requests to God" (NIV).

When I think about all that God did just to make it possible for us to be with him, I can't help but tear up. He is holy; our sin was our fault. He had every right to leave us in our brokenness or to hold us at arm's length, but he didn't! Instead, he scooped us up into his arms and said, *I am enough for you!*

I am so thankful we are on this journey together. Today remember what a priceless gift prayer is—a sign of your redemption and a proof of God's love for you.

Read Hebrews 10:19–22 out loud (yes, really, out loud!) and make it personal to you:

[I] have, then . . . complete freedom to go into the Most Holy Place by means of the death of Jesus. He opened for [me] a new way, a living way, through the curtain. . . . [I will] come near to God with a sincere heart and a sure faith, with [a heart] that [has] been purified from a guilty conscience. (GNT)

Good Enough

The LORD is gracious and merciful,
   slow to anger and abounding in steadfast love.
The LORD is good to all,
   and his mercy is over all that he has made.

PSALM 145:8–9 ESV

I was born a pastor's kid—a PK—and I was raised in church, as they say. From the time I was learning to walk, I was inside the church doors hours before the service started, and my family didn't leave until the last person said, "See you next week" and shook hands with my dad.

I was also born a sinner in need of God's grace.

When I was a young girl, I made the choice to follow Jesus. But then for years my understanding of sin far outweighed my understanding of God's grace. Sunday night church was a particularly painful event for me. That's when the invitation for those who needed to "get right with God" was given. Filled with shame and guilt, this pastor's daughter would admit once again that she had sinned. I might not have remembered any particular sin I had committed that week; I just knew I had *most likely* committed some sin that needed forgiving. So for years, because of my imbalanced theology and Satan's having a heyday with my overactive conscience, my prayer life consisted primarily of fear-filled requests, pleading with God to make me clean and good.

Does that sound at all familiar to you? That kind of grace is not very amazing, is it?

We often apply our experiences with authority figures to our relationship with God. For example, if you had a strict teacher as a child, you might tend to feel that God is corrective and exacting. It can also be challenging for those who grew up with absent or negative fathers to connect with God's personal and steadfast love. If this is true for you, I am so sorry. I wish I could reach through these pages and give you a hug.

Perhaps you had a wonderful family, but the unspoken pressures in this world and the constant weight of trying to be good has warped your view of God's unconditional grace. It takes intentional energy to change your default settings and your faith to believe that God's grace is enough to cover all your sin.

> It takes intentional energy to change your default settings and your faith to believe that God's grace is enough to cover all your sin.

If you're not sure if the conviction you feel is from God, here's how to tell: *conviction* from God leads us to repentance and reconciliation. It urges us to act and move toward growth, and ultimately it draws us deeper into his presence. Conviction is designed to motivate and excite us to want to spend time with God as our loving Father who invites us onto his lap—imperfections and all. However, *condemnation* drives us further away. It attacks our identity as children of God, and it stunts our growth and paralyzes our steps. Condemnation is not from God.

When we feel condemned, the problem is not as much our sinfulness as it is our understanding of God's grace. Your prayer life is not lacking because you don't pray; you, my friend, might be suffering from an anemic understanding of God's amazing grace.

On the days I realize I'm slipping into unhealthy and incorrect thinking, I choose to renew my mind with the truth of God's Word. You can too! Here are two of my favorite verses.

> There is no condemnation for those who belong to Christ Jesus. (Romans 8:1)

> If the Son [Jesus] sets you free, you are truly free. (John 8:36)

My dear, don't let a distorted view of God's grace hold you back from being in his presence—the very place you were born to be. Our God and King delights in you, and he cannot wait for you to draw nearer still to his heart.

———

The Bible is your guide when it comes to understanding your relationship with God and how he sees you. As you spend time with him today, consider these few creative ideas to help you focus on the truth of God's Word in Romans 8:1 and John 8:36.

- Underline and bookmark Romans 8:1 and John 8:36 in your Bible. You can even include the date and jot down some notes in the margin.
- Make one of these verses a lock screen for your phone or post it on one of your social media accounts.
- Write it down! Copy these verses onto a sticky note and post it on your bathroom mirror.

A Daughter's Cry

See how very much our Father loves us, for he calls us his children, and that is what we are!

1 JOHN 3:1

With knees and elbows bleeding and my six-year-old heart embarrassed by failure, I cried out "Daddy!" In an instant, my dad picked me up and held me close.

It was early Christmas morning, the smell of coffee and cinnamon in the air. Just minutes before, my scrawny little legs had been jumping up and down with excitement from discovering what had been hidden behind the Christmas tree in the night—a bright-red bicycle! My father had rescued it from a trash pile in the alley behind our house and lovingly transformed it into a Christmas gift worthy of the red bow on its handlebars. With delight and determination, we rolled it outside to the walkway, and I hopped onto the seat. With a kick of my heel, I took off down the path that ran along the front of our house and bent toward the street. And there, after missing the turn, I fell and landed in an icy puddle . . . to where my father came running at the sound of my cry.

My earthly father is an amazing dad, and he was displaying the heart of God that morning when he picked me up in his arms. But like every human father, he isn't perfect. And if I'm not careful, I can wrongly attach my version of a father figure—pieced together from his and other inadequate and imperfect examples around me— to my heavenly Father. In doing so, I taint my Father God's perfect love and care for me.

The word *Father* is one of the most frequently used words to describe God in the New Testament. Jesus himself uses it more than two hundred times. I can't help but agree with author Max Lucado, who said, "Of all his names, *Father* is God's favorite."[1] Yet depending on your experience, depending on the man or the men who exemplified fatherhood in your life, the very use of that name can evoke a host of emotions—some of which might be painful and in complete contradiction to the true meaning and heart of the word. It wasn't any different in Jesus's day. The distortion of the word *father* was in many ways even more extreme. During that time of Roman occupation, earthly fathers were legally permitted to beat and abuse their children.

So when Jesus described God as a loving father, it was on purpose and meant to provide us with a new and better picture. He wanted those listening to understand that God was a father like no other on earth. He was "Abba," a complete and perfect father to his children—kind, loving, gentle, and forgiving. Matchless in every way. Even though pop culture would want to demoralize the word *daddy*, it is by far one of the most endearing words used to describe an earthly father. *Daddy* is often the very first word a baby speaks. Dad is often the first person children cry out to when they need something. God is your good Father. You can cry out to "Daddy, Daddy!" anytime, anywhere—even when you are battered and bleeding or feel embarrassed and ashamed—and he will come running, ready to hold you close in his arms.

Perhaps your earthly father has failed you. He might have been absent or neglectful or even caused you harm. If so, God wants to redefine fatherhood for you. He wants you to experience what true fatherhood is. He wants to be a dad to you like you've never had before, one who astounds you with his unconditional love.

> **God wants to redefine fatherhood for you. He wants you to experience what true fatherhood is.**

Just as a young father's heart skips a beat when he hears his baby girl's voice, so God, your heavenly Father, is thrilled when he hears you call out to him. He cannot wait to speak to you, to hear you say his name. He longs to hear from you, his daughter. You delight his heart. Galatians 4:6 says, "You can tell for sure that you are now fully adopted as his own children because God sent the Spirit of his Son into our lives crying out, 'Papa! Father!'" (MSG).

You were created to have a close and intimate relationship with your heavenly Father. He wants you to call out to him when you're in trouble and whenever you're looking for comfort or reassurance or you need his guidance.

At first, it might feel uncomfortable for you to relate so intimately with the God of the universe as a father. But that is exactly what he desires. He wants you, his beloved and precious child, to step into this beautiful father-daughter dance with him.

In your journal or in the space provided, write a letter to your heavenly Father. Open your heart to him as a daughter would, and then tell him what his perfect and matchless love means to you.

Let's Talk

They heard the sound of the LORD God walking in the garden in the cool of the day.

GENESIS 3:8 ESV

I was so nervous. I had just met him a month before. John, the cutest guy in the church youth group, the one who had already proven himself to be a big flirt, had asked me on a date! And there he was standing at the door, looking way cool with his wavy, sun-kissed hair and wire-rimmed sunglasses. And after some loving parental reminders about driving carefully and being home on time, we were off, just the two of us, in his midnight-blue Pontiac Firebird.

Did I mention how nervous I was—*eek!* What if we didn't have enough to talk about? But I shouldn't have worried. As we slid into the booth tucked in the back corner of the Pizza Hut, we were already talking with ease. We did manage to pause our conversation long enough to order a pepperoni pan pizza and two Cokes, but we talked for hours on that first date. We asked each other questions about all sorts of things—big and little, serious and funny. My curiosity was off the charts. I wanted to know everything about him!

That was just the beginning. Soon we were talking on the phone every day—again for hours. I'm sure our conversations would sound like endless small talk to others—trivial, even—but to us, what we discussed was important stuff. We wanted to know every detail about each other's day and thoughts. John wanted to get to know me, and I wanted to get to know him. Every conversation seemed like a big deal.

I look back on those days and smile. John and I were both just sixteen years old on that first date, and today, forty years later, we're still talking. We just had breakfast. He made scrambled eggs and ham, and as we sat next to each other and talked about that first conversation, we laughed. I could have talked to him for hours this morning, but we both had to get to work!

This reminds me of the long conversations I imagine Adam and Eve had with God when they walked in the garden. The book of Genesis tells us they walked together every day as the sun set and the grass cooled. I wonder what they talked about and laughed about, and I wonder what questions Eve asked God and what his answers were.

How incredible is it that we get to do that very thing with God! We have talked about how he is a father to us, but God is also a friend. In prayer, we can speak to him as our friend. Through prayer, we share our heart with God and he shares his with us.

I love how this verse puts it:

> God-friendship is for God-worshipers;
> They are the ones he confides in. (Psalm 25:14 MSG).

Like a close friend, God is deeply interested in you and your life. I don't think Adam and Eve were the only ones who asked questions during those evening strolls.

We might think that, because God is omniscient and knows everything, he isn't interested in hearing about our days or our thoughts. But God is profoundly interested in relationship, and so he is fascinated by your thoughts, your wishes, your hopes, and your dreams because everything about you is important to him. A mother already knows everything there is to know about her toddler's day—what she did, what he ate and if he liked it—but she still longs for her child to talk with her. She wants to hear the dramatized play-by-play of their day because she's invested in the relationship. It's true that God already knows everything about us, but relationship makes his heart sing, and so he wants us to tell him everything, including our concerns, worries, and anxieties.

Listen to what Psalm 37:23 says: "The LORD directs the steps of the godly. He delights in *every detail* of their lives" (emphasis mine). Let that thought sink in. In the same way God never tires of the sun rising or setting, he never gets tired of your everyday conversations. He wants to be an active part of your world. He doesn't become irritated when you ask the same questions again. No, he is fully invested in your friendship—a relationship that is meant to be growing and deepening through every conversation with him.

> **In the same way God never tires of the sun rising or setting, he never gets tired of your everyday conversations.**

The more John and I talked, the more we understood each other. The more we talked, the deeper our affection grew for each other. The more time we spent together, the more our conversations matured and deepened. And the same is true for your relationship with God. The more you spend time talking with him, the more you'll learn about his character and his love for you.

God longs for relationship with you. Yes, you specifically. He has been calling you to draw near and talk to him. Maybe that's why you're reading this right now. And he is reaching out to you still, longing for you to sit and chat with him, perhaps over breakfast.

Psalm 27:8 says, "My heart has heard you say, 'Come and talk with me.' And my heart responds, 'LORD, I am coming.'"

In your prayer time today, I encourage you to just chat with God. Tell him about your day, about whatever is on your mind. Your conversations with him don't have to be formal and serious. Enjoy talking with him like you would enjoy talking to a close and trusted friend.

Three in One

May the grace of the Lord Jesus Christ, the love of God, and the fellowship of the Holy Spirit be with you all.

2 CORINTHIANS 13:14

Not long ago I was with a group of girls who had traveled with me on a mission trip. We had a wonderful time rejoicing in all that God had done, each of them sharing stories of how he had used that little team to touch the world.

Toward the end of our time together, I asked several of them around the circle to pray out loud for specific needs that had been shared. I didn't know that one of the girls I chose had never prayed out loud in a group setting. When her turn came, there was a long pause as she shyly looked around the room. And then with innocent abandon she blurted, "I don't know if this is right, but here it goes. Dear God . . ." And then with heartfelt words, she presented her request to him. Her prayer was simply addressed to "God"—beautifully innocent, direct, and bursting with faith. I'm pretty sure God thought it was perfect!

Her prayer reminds me of a question girls often ask: "Who should I talk to when I pray?" They want to know if they should say "Dear God" or pray to the Father or to Jesus. "And what about the Holy Spirit?" they ask. *Who should I talk to when I pray?* is a great question, and I believe it deserves exploration.

Often our backgrounds and experiences shape our understanding of prayer rather than our knowledge of what the Bible teaches. And just like when the disciple said, "Lord, teach us," it's good for us to say the same when it comes to this question.

The Bible refers to the Father, Son, and Holy Spirit as one God yet separate, distinct persons, all with differing roles. The great mystery of one God in three persons is known as the doctrine of the Trinity, and it is a unique characteristic of our God. No religion other than Christianity has a concept like it. Simply put, the Trinity is one God in three equal persons—the Father, the Son, and the Holy Spirit. All three are separate yet perfectly reliant on the other two. They work together seamlessly and in constant delight with one another. And all three persons are equally and deeply invested in their relationship with us.

When we pray, we join a conversation already taking place between all the members of the Trinity. We are swept up in this divine union—adopted, accepted, and listened to as the children of God we are. Second Peter 1:4 expresses this thought so beautifully: "Because of his glory and excellence, he has given us great and precious promises. These are the promises that enable you to share his divine nature." Through God's promises and our position of acceptance, we are given the gift to share in "his divine nature" and contribute to the beautiful conversation with our own words!

> When we pray, we join a conversation already taking place between all the members of the Trinity.

The truth is that when you pray, you are connecting to all of God's nature, the entire Trinity—the Father, Jesus the Son, and the Holy Spirit—who all intimately and equally love you and hear you. Yet depending on your upbringing, your knowledge of God's divine character, or what you were taught, you might feel as though you relate more easily to one part of the Trinity than to the others. Many of us have been taught to begin our prayers a certain way. Or just by listening to other believers praying around us, we have adopted a certain way of praying.

Although God understands we are all growing in our knowledge of who he is and in what it means to have a personal and vibrant relationship with him, when it comes to prayer and how we interact with his divine "three in one" character, we should all want to know what the Bible teaches us.

First, no rivalry or jealousy exists between the three persons of God. If you call out to Jesus for help, as did the thief on the cross in Luke 23:42, God the Father does not gasp in dismay and say, "Why does she like Jesus more than me?" Or if you say, "Holy Spirit, lead me today," Jesus and the Father are not bothered. Why? Because they are all one and the same. That being said, Jesus taught on this very topic, and prayer was an integral part of his everyday life on earth. He prayed regularly. He prayed for others, he prayed for himself, he prayed in public, and he prayed alone. Prayer was important to him, and the how of prayer was a part of his teaching. He wanted his followers to understand how to pray. And since Jesus came to earth to be our example, it's important for us to pay attention when he gives us a model to follow.

In approaching God in prayer, Jesus himself was purposeful. He was also specific in his teaching to the disciples. He taught clearly that they should approach God like this: "When you pray . . . pray to your Father" (Matthew 6:6), and then again he said, "This, then, is how you should pray: 'Our Father . . .'" (verse 9 NIV). Not only did he teach this to his disciples, but every time Jesus himself prayed, he addressed God as his "heavenly Father."

It's interesting to consider that even though Jesus was fully God and understood the nature of God and the role of the Holy Spirit, he did not say, "Take your pick. Pray to any one of us." He wanted the disciples to grasp the importance of praying to God as their Father and to fully realize that they were to bring glory to his name in their conversations with him. Remember, Jesus was the one who made the way for us to have access to our heavenly Father. He wants you and me not only to understand the incredible privilege we have in approaching God for our needs but to also understand that in submitting to the Father, through the name of Jesus, we connect to his divine will.

Now, it's important for you to see that although Jesus clearly taught a certain model of prayer, the Bible indicates your prayers are heard whether you call out to the Father, to Jesus the Son, or to the Holy Spirit. It's not wrong for you to speak to Jesus as your friend, to sing to him and to praise both him and the Holy Spirit for who they are and all they do in your life. Yet as you process this thought today, I encourage you to think about what Jesus taught and practiced himself and to consider directing your devotional prayers and requests to the Father, in the name of Jesus.

Just like when the girl prayed "Dear God" out loud for the first time, when you look to your heavenly Father in prayer with daughter-like faith, he is ready to hear and respond to your voice—no matter what!

Remember how in Day 3, "A Curtain Torn," we looked at how Jesus made a way for you to have a relationship with the Father? Consider how what Jesus did relates to how you approach the Father in prayer.

One of my favorite worship songs is "Behold" from the album *Let There Be Light* by Hillsong Worship. I encourage you to listen to that song during your prayer time and to consider the uniqueness of God's divine nature and how it relates to your relationship with him.

For further study, I recommend the book *Delighting in the Trinity* by Michael Reeves.

A Secret Place

Jesus often withdrew to the wilderness for prayer.

LUKE 5:16

Today I'm going to get a bit more personal with you. I want to talk about your personal prayer and devotional time with God. At some point you might have heard the phrase "quiet time with God" or "having devotions" from a Christian friend or a pastor. Maybe you've wondered what exactly that means. Does the Bible teach that we need to personally and individually "be with God" in a certain way or at a certain time of day? Does going to church count as "my time with God"?

First, I remind you that being a Christian isn't based on a list of rules and methods. Being a Christian is based on a loving and voluntary relationship with God, your heavenly Father. You chose to surrender your life to follow him, and he chose to accept and forgive you because he loves you. Your love for him and his love for you are personal and real. And just as with any earthly loving relationship, your relationship with God takes time, attention, and intimate interaction with him to flourish and grow and to stay strong and healthy.

This means we don't spend time with God because he demands it or requires it; we spend time with him because we love him and desire to know him better, our hearts longing daily to be united with his heart and thoughts toward us. When we're in his presence, we can interact personally with God, enjoying and receiving all that he offers and provides: through our heavenly Father, his power to help with everything we seek (1 John 5:14); through Jesus our Savior, friendship (John 15:15); and through the Holy Spirit, counseling, comforting, and teaching (John 14:16).

When I think of all that God offers us through his divine character, I am in awe! And it makes me more aware of why I want to be in his presence every day.

The more I grow in my relationship with God, the more my soul craves quiet space *alone* with him. Being with him and focusing my attention on him are imperative to keeping my heart at rest, my soul refreshed, and my thoughts in tune with his will. Bottom line, I need him more than ever and I want to be with him!

This morning when I woke up, I so longed to be with him, to be enveloped by his love and grace. I was determined to find a quiet place away from every distraction. So I grabbed my Bible, and then I got into my car and turned on some worship music. Then God and I went for a ride and watched the sun come up. It was so incredible. His presence was precious and real. As I worshipped him and shared my thoughts and needs with him, my soul was strengthened and renewed. I came home thirty minutes later to start my busy day with fresh faith and confidence that God was going to help me with what I needed to do.

My husband and I live busy lives as leaders of a growing church family, and we're also the grandparents of eight little ones who all live within a ten-minute drive of our house. Life is a constant whirlwind. It's all exciting and loads of fun, but to be honest, sometimes it's hard. Life is just plain busy!

I love being Grandma. I also love leading and connecting with people. I have the kind of personality that thrives on a busy schedule. I crave variety. I'm an enthusiastic extrovert by nature, and I love to make people happy! And if at all possible, I find a way to sprinkle an element of fun into everything. My motto is "The more people and confetti, the better!"

But sometimes it can be a challenge to juggle all the aspects of sustaining a healthy ministry (leadership responsibilities, attending meetings); my speaking and writing; and maintaining a healthy personal life (enjoying time with family and friends, being Grandma, working out, reading the books on my nightstand, and on and on).

Your life might not look exactly like mine, but I bet you could say the same—life is just plain busy! Finding and having intentional quiet time with God (not just drive-by-and-wave moments with him) can easily be pushed to the edge of the day and fall over the cliff.

Yes, we can talk to God anywhere—and we don't even need a cell phone to do it. I am so thankful for that! We can pray in Walmart or at the park. We can pray in geometry class or in the middle of a job interview.

God is ready to hear your whispered prayer, even when you're on the go or surrounded by a crowd of people. But as a lover of God, you should long to reach a higher level—a place where you purposefully create space and time to be alone, just you and him. No distractions.

The conversations John and I have alone as a couple—just the two of us, apart from everything and everyone else—take on a more intimate tone. That's how it is meant to be. When we're in a crowd, even if we're trying to have a deep and personal conversation, we can be distracted and interrupted by what is going on around us. But when we are alone together, focused on each other, we have the space to dig deeper into each other's heart, to freely share our intimate thoughts and feelings.

Conversely, if John and I never purposed to spend time alone together, our ability to easily connect and communicate would become more and more difficult and our relationship would eventually become superficial—or even worse. When you love someone, you want to be with them. You long to share times of deep, personal connection. You crave to be with them, to hear their voice. And that is how it should be with your Father God, the one who loves you most.

In the book of Psalms, David often shared about his longing for time with God. In Psalm 63:1 he wrote, "O God, You are my God; I shall seek You earnestly; My soul thirsts for You, my flesh yearns for You, in a dry and weary land where there is no water" (NASB). You can sense David's passion, his desire and his deep longing, from his words. It's as though his very life depends on being in God's presence. And that is the point.

Even Jesus longed for time alone in the presence of his Father. Luke 5:16 says, "Jesus Himself would often slip away to the wilderness and pray [in seclusion]" (NASB).

Think about that. His work was literally to save people spiritually. He must have felt the pressure to keep working, teaching, healing, and comforting these desperate people. Yet Jesus regularly left the crowds behind and escaped to a quiet place to pray. This is fascinating to me. I mean, who would imagine that Jesus would need and long for time alone with God? He *was* God, after all. Yet he did. He made it a priority for himself, and he taught the importance of it to the disciples.

Here's what Jesus said about this in his own words: "Here's what I want you to do: Find a quiet, secluded place. . . . Just be there as simply and honestly as you can manage. The focus will shift from you to God, and you will begin to sense his grace. . . . This is your Father you are dealing with, and he knows better than you what you need. With a God like this loving you, you can pray very simply" (Matthew 6:6–9 MSG). If Jesus wanted it, I want it too.

I know it can seem nearly impossible to find time and space to be with God, especially if you have a demanding job, a crazy schedule, or little ones who need your constant care. Still, I encourage you to creatively find a place to begin. (Even pray about it!) Maybe you can have ten minutes of quiet prayer before the kids get up or during your drive to work. Or maybe you can set aside your lunch break to be alone with God. Jeremiah 29:12–13 says, "'When you pray, I will listen. If you look for me wholeheartedly, you will find me. I will be found by you,' says the LORD."

————————

It can be challenging to get into the habit of spending intentional devotional time with God. I encourage you to take these steps to make spending time with him easy and inviting!

- Choose a time that makes the most sense for you to carve out a few minutes to be with God—morning, evening, or sometime in between.
- Find a comfy spot in your home to go to every day. Maybe it's a favorite chair, the kitchen table, or on the floor surrounded by your favorite pillows. Make it cozy! I love to light a candle and play worship music.
- Place your Bible within easy reach, along with a notebook or journal and a pen.
- Make a cup of coffee or your favorite tea and enjoy your "secret place."

SHE PRAYS
Knowled

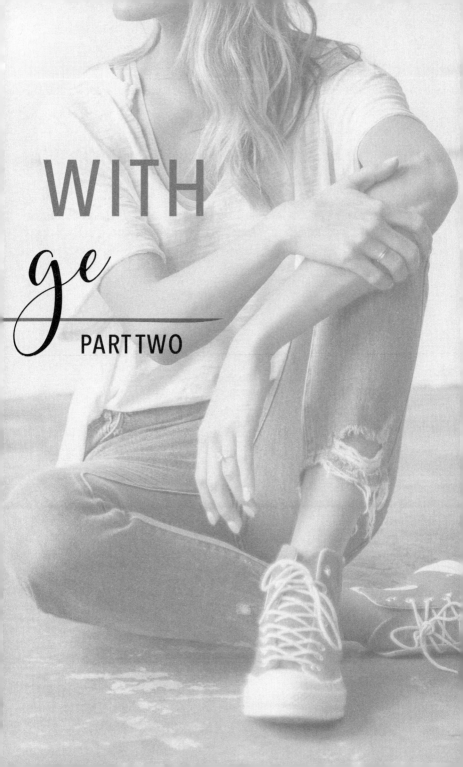

More to Learn

One of his disciples said to him, "Lord, teach us to pray."

LUKE 11:1 ESV

No matter where you are on your prayer journey, whether you're just starting out or you've been in conversation with the Father for decades, you have more to learn. And that should be exciting news. God has more for you!

When Jesus walked the earth, his close followers wanted to learn more. Watching Jesus pray made them want to become better and more effective in how they communicated with their heavenly Father. Have you ever been around someone who makes you want to pray better? I have. My dear friend Estella Clark is in heaven now, but when she was here with us, she prayed up a storm. Her power-packed sincerity was what made it seem like she was touching God's hand, not how loud her voice was or how long her prayers were.

Luke 11 tells us that one day, after Jesus had finished praying, one of his disciples (obviously, the brave one) walked over to him and said, "Lord, teach us to pray." Now, this guy was one of Jesus's close disciples; he had walked, eaten, traveled, and ministered alongside Jesus—literally. Time and time again, he had been amazed by the miracles performed before his eyes. He heard Jesus speak "Be healed" over a man suffering from leprosy and then watched the sores on the man disappear. He had witnessed a broken and crippled body transform into perfect wholeness right before his eyes. He had looked on in wonder when Jesus fed more than five thousand people with two little fish and five loaves of bread. He listened to Jesus pray day after day. Yet I imagine a desire rose up inside him so strong that he couldn't sit still any longer. So he mustered up the nerve to ask Jesus for help.

I love his boldness and his desire. I love how he said, "Teach us," not "Teach me." He knew his request would benefit his friends as well.

But this disciple didn't ask for a lesson on healing. He didn't say, "Jesus, please show us the secret for how to perform a miracle." What captivated his attention most and what he was jealous to understand was the way Jesus prayed. In walking beside him day in and day out, he recognized that Jesus's ability to submit to God's will, his astounding wisdom, and his supernatural power all flowed from one thing: his deep and personal relationship with his Father God.

Can you and I say the same? Do we recognize that the most important thing we can learn as believers is how to communicate with our Creator God? Do we realize that everything Jesus experienced through his relationship with his Father God is ours as well to embrace and enjoy?

You can never achieve or possess or buy any knowledge that will have a greater impact on your life. Jesus knew that our prayer life affects everything—every circumstance we face, every difficulty we walk through, every relationship we need help with. Prayer provides both wisdom to know what to do and answers for the questions we face. It gives us guidance for the future. Jesus knew prayer is what connects the believer to the power and wisdom of God.

As you and I, just like the disciples, look to Jesus to teach us, he delights in gently and graciously leading us into a fuller understanding and a greater confidence in prayer. Everything Jesus is and has is yours. Even now, his passion is to take you by the hand and lead you into our Father's presence, to pray down blessings and reveal the will of heaven in your life, your home, your work, and your calling.

I want to have the heart of a learner. I want to be sure I never come to a place where I feel like I have arrived in prayer. I want to be a disciple who kneels at the feet of Jesus and asks, "Lord,

> **Prayer provides both wisdom to know what to do and answers for the questions we face. It gives us guidance for the future.**

teach me to pray." I want to continue to grow deeper in my understanding of how, through prayer, I can connect to the heart of the Father, submit to his will with complete surrender, and see his power visibly at work in my life. I want to know him better and understand his heart more every day. And that is what I want for you.

The well is deep and wide and full of unending blessings. Together, let's reach down deep into that well to learn all that God has for us. He's ready and willing to guide you into deeper communion with him.

You've already reached Day 9 of our prayer journey together, and you obviously have a desire to grow and learn. I love that! Look back over your prayer journey. In

71

what ways has your prayer life grown since you became a Christian?

Today I encourage you to think about how you specifically want to grow now. Maybe you want to pray with more confidence, believing at a deeper level that God is listening and willing to respond to you. Maybe you want to grow in your boldness in praying out loud around others. Maybe, like the disciples, you desire to see the supernatural at work in a greater way through your prayers. Write down what you want God to teach you and ask him to reveal more to your heart. I promise, he will respond and help you grow.

your Father

I will be a father to you, and you shall be sons and daughters to me, says the Lord Almighty.

2 CORINTHIANS 6:18 ESV

Before Jesus came to earth, nobody called God their Father. None of the biblical figures understood what their relationship with God was fully meant to be. When sin entered the world, it diminished the personal connection God desired to share with humanity. Only through the life, death, and resurrection of Jesus are we able to claim our redeemed identities as children of God.

Jesus introduced us to the Father. In the Sermon on the Mount (Matthew 5–7), Jesus referred to God as Father three times. He clearly wanted his listeners to realize that they, like him, were meant to have a very personal relationship with the one he himself called Father. Galatians 4:4–5 says, "When the fullness of time had come, God sent forth his Son, born of woman, born under the law, to redeem those who were under the law, so that we might receive adoption as sons" (ESV).

Our adoption into God's family means we don't need to feel like intruders in his sacred space. We never need to feel apologetic when we pray. We are not servants bound to work without any of the freedom and blessings given to the children of the master. No, we are the children of the King. Galatians 4:4–7 says, "You can tell for sure that you are now fully adopted as his own children because God sent the Spirit of his Son into our lives crying out, 'Papa! Father!' Doesn't that privilege of intimate conversation with God make it plain that you are not a slave, but a child? And if you are a child, you're also an heir, with complete access to the inheritance" (MSG).

When I was seven years old, my parents adopted my sister. They brought Sue home when she was just a few days old, and I immediately fell in love with her. I would hold her for hours, play with her, and teach her things as she learned to talk, then walk, then run. But our love wasn't enough to give her the sense of belonging she needed. Though we loved her fiercely, love wasn't what made the adoption final and the privileges that came with it hers. What gave her the surety of legal, emotional, relational, and spiritual membership in our family was the act of adoption. Through a legal process, my parents signed documents, confirming before witnesses that my sister was officially part of our family.

Adoption empowered my sister with full citizenship, with a right to all the blessings, gifts, resources, companionship, and love and hugs my brother and I shared. And no one—and nothing—could take that away from her.

What does this have to do with prayer? Everything. Your prayer life will flourish and your relationship with God will mature when you believe in the deep and abiding love of your heavenly Father. When you are secure in knowing who you are and can say with complete assurance, *I am a child of God; I belong to him*, your prayers will be transformed. You will become bolder and more confident in the way you approach God.

You are God's daughter! You have a heavenly Father you can trust to be there for you whenever you call on him and who loves you more than you could ever imagine.

You might say, *How can I be sure of this? It seems too good to be true!* The proof, my friend, is in plain sight: "You received God's Spirit when he adopted you as his own children. Now we call him, 'Abba, Father.' For his Spirit joins with our spirit to affirm that we are God's children. And since we are his children, we are his heirs.

In fact, together with Christ we are heirs of God's glory" (Romans 8:15–17). So your spirit bears witness that you are a daughter of God. And when you became a Christian, God confirmed your adoption and sealed your soul with the mark of his Holy Spirit. You have been officially adopted, my dear. Legalized, ratified, immutable. No one and nothing can ever take that away from you.

> You have full citizenship in the family of God. You are forever his child.

You have full citizenship in the family of God. You are forever his child. You now have a heavenly Father who claims you as his own.

Every conversation you have with God starts and flows from this father-daughter relationship. All your requests and thoughts, the vibrancy and depth of your prayer life, hang on this incredible truth: *God is your Father, and you are forever his beloved daughter.* The question is, How strongly do you believe that? Does the way you pray reflect your identity as a daughter to your heavenly Father?

What does it mean to you that God is your true Father? What words come to mind when you think about your adoption into God's family? How does this change your thoughts and perspective about your earthly family, your work, your calling, your passion to serve him?

Today, as a statement of belief in your heavenly adoption, personalize the verse in 2 Corinthians 6:18 by writing your name in the blank: "I will be a father to you, and _____ shall be [a daughter] to me, says the Lord Almighty" (ESV).

Touching Earth

**The LORD has established his throne in the heavens,
and his kingdom rules over all.**

PSALM 103:19 ESV

When studying the Lord's Prayer in Matthew 6, I found
myself asking, *Why did Jesus choose to include the four
words "who is in heaven"?* He could have skipped them
and just said, "Our Father, hallowed be your name."
What would have been lost if this phrase hadn't been
in the prayer? Why make the point of God's dwelling
place? What did it mean for us? As I considered my
questions, I loved what the Lord revealed to my heart:
Jesus knew his disciples intimately, exactly as God
knows human nature inside and out.

He knew we would tend to think of our relationship with our heavenly Father through the lens of our relationships with human beings on earth and that the nature and character of those closest to us would become the template for how we viewed him. It's our default setting. And in this statement Jesus was making the distinction between earthly human character and the divine and perfect character of our Father in heaven.

The best of friends will eventually let us down somehow, and the best parents always have their blind spots. Those we talk with, work with, and live with don't always help us grow into the people we are meant to be. Because we're human, not one of us has the ability to love perfectly—only God can do that.

I am so thankful that God operates on a different level. Where human relationships fail, God steps in. When people give up on us, he offers a second chance. And where we push each other toward earthly success, God points toward spiritual growth: "I am God, and there is no other; I am God, and there is no one like Me" (Isaiah 46:9 NASB).

Praying to God in heaven reminds us that he is omniscient, all-knowing, and omnipotent, all-powerful. He transcends all earthly limitations. What is impossible for us in this world is just a normal task for God. He is the Almighty, and his power isn't bound by any structure, rule, or system that exists on earth. We can't begin to comprehend how the power that upholds the cosmos is the same power that gives us strength for today. We don't even have the words to describe just how much bigger, higher, stronger, and more powerful God is. He says, "I am GOD, the God of everything living. Is there anything I can't do?" (Jeremiah 32:27 MSG).

What is impossible for us in this world is just a normal task for God.

God's ways are not our ways, and heaven is not earth. Different rules apply to the kingdom of God than apply in the world of men. The phrase *who is in heaven* calls us to remember that God is wholly "other" than us and our world. He is not human, and human rules do not apply to him. And yet, at the same time, we are also reminded that God doesn't just stay in heaven. He is not far removed. Oh no, he came down to live among us. In the person of Christ and through the continued work of the Holy Spirit, heaven touches earth. John 14 tells us that God does not leave us here alone like orphans. And God himself says, "Shout and rejoice, O beautiful Jerusalem, for I am coming to live among you. . . . I will live among you, and you will know that the LORD of Heaven's Armies sent me to you" (Zechariah 2:10–11). Romans 8:11 says, "The Spirit of God, who raised Jesus from the dead, lives in you."

If those four little words—*who is in heaven*—hadn't been included in the Lord's Prayer, I'm sure it would be far too easy for us to think and speak to God in worldly terms with earthly limitations in mind. They remind us who God truly is, that his ways and his thoughts are unlike anything we know on earth. Isaiah 55:8–9 says, "'My thoughts are nothing like your thoughts,' says the LORD. 'And my ways are far beyond anything you could imagine. For just as the heavens are higher than the earth, so my ways are higher than your ways and my thoughts higher than your thoughts.'"

Understanding that God is heavenly, that his character is above all and over all, motivates our faith to believe in his power as we pray! The beautifully stunning truth is that we pray to the God who is altogether complete in every way, who has all authority, whose presence unfolds beyond the edges of the cosmos—and yet he permeates our very souls. How truly marvelous it is that we can talk with him in prayer. What a gift it is to have an intimate relationship with him while we're here on earth.

And really, this is the marvel of Jesus—God's Son, perfect in every way, coming to earth to redeem us—and the truth that makes every day of the year meaningful: God, who is divine and otherworldly, is at the same time, now and always, here with us and in us. This heavenly God, who exists beyond anything we can describe, came down to fit himself into humanity to heal our brokenness, mend our souls, and invite us into relationship with him.

In your prayer time today, think about what it means for you to have a relationship with the God in heaven as you read John 1:14: "So the Word became human and made his home among us. He was full of unfailing love and faithfulness. And we have seen his glory, the glory of the Father's one and only Son." Repeat the verse to yourself a few times, letting your mind linger on how a righteous and holy God stooped into our humanity to reveal his divine, extravagant love for us.

What's His Name?

**Those who know your name trust in you,
for you, O LORD, do not abandon those who search
for you.**

PSALM 9:10

Names had great significance in Bible times. A person's name told you where they were from, their family background, and their social status. It could even tell that individual's religious beliefs and their occupation. A name gave you an understanding of who the person was and how you could respond to them.

It's the same with your heavenly Father's name. The more you know his name, the more you know all that his being and character encompass—the weight of his holiness.

John Piper writes that "only a tenth of his character is given to us in this age for our contemplation, and even this is so great that we will never exhaust its riches."[1] God's name is holy because it is everything beautiful, powerful, and precious. And we hallow his name—honor his name—when we believe and trust in him.

In the book of Exodus, we read the story of a man named Moses. God tells Moses he is sending him to rescue the Israelites from slavery in Egypt. To Moses's thinking, this is an impossible task, and he tells God he doesn't have the authority to make Pharaoh release the slaves. He asks who he is to do this. After all, nobody will listen to little old Moses. God agrees. Moses can't go in the power of his own name. But then God reminds Moses that he is sent in the power of *God's* name: "Say this to the people of Israel: I AM has sent me to you" (Exodus 3:14 ESV). His message is clear: "Don't worry about who you are or what you're capable of, Moses. Trust in who I AM."

God is the creator of the cosmos, the eternal one, self-defining, self-sustaining, utterly and immutably perfect. In God's name, the impossible becomes possible. In him we find protection and help. Proverbs 18:10 says, "The name of the LORD is a strong fortress; the godly run to him and are safe."

How often do we rely on ourselves and on our own names rather than on the power and salvation available to us in the name of the Lord? As Romans 10:13 says, "Everyone who calls on the name of the Lord will be saved" (ESV).

Moses is one of the most revered biblical figures because of how much he relied on God. He spent a lot of time in his presence. And the more time he spent getting to know God, the more he understood God's character. Some time after he received his mission to liberate the slaves, Moses hiked to the top of a mountain to spend time in prayer. God gave him an even fuller under-standing of his holy name. He said, "Yahweh! The LORD! The God of compassion and mercy! I am slow to anger and filled with unfailing love and faithfulness. I lavish un-failing love to a thousand generations. I forgive iniquity, rebellion, and sin. But I do not excuse the guilty" (Exodus 34:6–7). This is such a profound verse to me because God is talking about himself. This is how he introduces himself. This is the God you and I get to know through prayer.

As with Moses, the more we spend time with God, the more we'll understand who he is. We give him honor and praise when we believe and trust in what he says about himself.

When we enter God's presence in prayer, we have to re-member that we are stepping onto holy ground. When we pray in God's holy name, we draw near to his holy power. What does it mean to *hallow* his name? The word simply means to honor as holy. It means to treat God as he truly is with all the reverence he deserves. It means to *believe* in his name.

> **When we pray in God's holy name, we draw near to his holy power.**

Like Moses learned to trust in God's powerful name, we must learn to trust that God will do what he says and that what he says is true. First John 5:10 tells us, "Whoever does not believe God has made him a liar" (ESV). If we enter prayer without the belief that God is who he says he is, we insult his identity, his power, and his love for us. When we let our human fear override God's truth, we don't hallow his name. God's name is not honored when we don't have peace or faith in the one to whom we pray.

But when we hold in our hearts that what God has spoken is true, we give him honor. As John Piper said, "'Hallowed be your name' means 'Trusted be your word.'"[2]

Consider ways you might be striving to do things in the power of your own name. How might God be calling you to rely on his name for what you need his help with today? I encourage you to listen to the song "No Other Name" by Hillsong Worship during your prayer time, and as you do, to thank God for what his name means for you.

What's His Name?

87

The Forecast Is Reign

All that is in the heavens and in the earth is yours. Yours is the kingdom, O LORD, and you are exalted as head above all.

1 CHRONICLES 29:11 ESV

A key message of Jesus's ministry was to proclaim that the kingdom of God is coming. He's quoted talking about the kingdom more than a hundred times in the Gospel narratives, and he often said, "The kingdom of God is at hand."

What did he mean by that? And why does it relate to our prayers?

To gain some clarity, let's talk about what the kingdom of God is *not*. It's not really a physical place. God, angels, our own souls—all spiritual things have influence in the physical world, but they're not restricted to it. We understand from Scripture that God is the Creator and ruler of both the physical and the spiritual world. He—singular—sits and rules on the throne! Everything is under his authority and ownership, including our world. He influences and reshapes it at will.

In the beginning of time, God's reign and our world coexisted. They overlapped perfectly. This is pictured in the garden of Eden, Genesis 2, where God and humans worked together in tandem and humans lived in peace with each other and with nature. Genesis 2:25 says, "The man and his wife were both naked, but they felt no shame." (Okay, just to be honest right here, I struggle with a bit of garden of Eden envy. Imagine how much time we would have to pray if we didn't have to get dressed every day!)

Back to reality. I know it's difficult to wrap our minds around what it would be like if our world and God's reign overlapped today. How would the earth be different if sin had never entered the picture? Unfortunately, that perfect union between God and man didn't last very long. Satan enticed Adam and Eve through the one thing he knew would tempt them—their pride. Soon after God blew his breath in them to give them life, humans decided they didn't want to live under the reign of the Creator and opted to go their own way. They preferred their own egos rather than God's divine power and wisdom. So out of respect for our free will—for God did not want slaves but willing followers—he let them do what they wanted. God's reign and the beautiful world he created no longer coexisted. Now we have two kingdoms: Satan's kingdom of pride, false power, hatred, greed, and selfishness and God's kingdom of humility, true divine power, unconditional love, and mercy.

When the apostle Paul wrote to the first generation of Christians, he clarified the divide between the kingdoms when he told them that the kingdom of this world is "headed for destruction. Their god is their appetite, they brag about shameful things, and they think only about this life here on earth. *But we are citizens of heaven, where the Lord Jesus Christ lives. And we are eagerly waiting for him to return as our Savior*" (Philippians 3:19–20, emphasis mine).

Paul confirms the stark difference between the two kingdoms—one is light and the other is darkness. The kingdom of darkness is seductive and evil. We see the results of this darkness in the pain and brokenness that surround us. We hear the lies and false promises of this kingdom every day, and it can be difficult to remember that we have a higher calling as citizens of the kingdom of light. We need to constantly remind ourselves that by intentionally seeking God's kingdom through prayer, we can bring the light of God's love to a world in need.

When we pray, we're working to strengthen and expand God's kingdom here on earth, his rule, his power, and his grace. When we say, "God, your kingdom come," we're proclaiming his authority and our desire for Jesus's return, when sin and death will be no more and God's kingdom will reign supreme over all. Like an explorer marking new territories with the flag of his country, we are reclaiming territory from the Enemy, putting a stake in the ground over our lives, our families, our marriages, our dreams, and our future—a future ruled by the light of God's glory. As Revelation 11:15 says, "Then the seventh angel blew his trumpet, and there were loud voices in heaven, saying, 'The kingdom of the world has become the kingdom of our Lord and of his Christ, and he shall reign forever and ever'"(ESV). *Amen!*

> When we pray, we're working to strengthen and expand God's kingdom here on earth, his rule, his power, and his grace.

Jesus said, "Fear not, little flock, for it is your Father's good pleasure to give you the kingdom" (Luke 12:32 ESV). Take time to meditate on this verse and consider how it relates to you and your time in God's presence. How do the words *give you the kingdom* encourage your heart and mind?

_____

_____

_____

_____

_____

_____

_____

_____

_____

_____

_____

_____

_____

Matter of Wills

DAY 14

"My thoughts are nothing like your thoughts," says
    the LORD.
  "And my ways are far beyond anything you could
    imagine."

ISAIAH 55:8

I had always believed it was God's will for us to have
four children. But that dream came to a halt after our
third child, Savannah, was born. After nearly dying in
childbirth and with my body weak from either being
pregnant or nursing for thirty-six consecutive months,
my doctor recommended that John and I stop having
children. Since we loved having sex (yes, I just said that
word in a devotional), we opted for the doctor's sugges-
tion of a permanent-solution procedure. It was a hard

decision for me, but I knew it was the right one. I was just twenty-four years old, and I wanted to be strong and healthy for the three children God had given us.

Still, I wasn't ready to give up on my dream of a family with four children. So over the next ten years, we made several attempts to adopt. But every time the adoptions fell through. Then one day after months of seeking an answer, we were approved to adopt a teenage mother's baby. This little guy would be another Lindell boy! As we walked with the mother through the first five months of her pregnancy, John and I talked endlessly about what we should name him and how he was going to be the perfect addition to our family. I was so excited.

But then, out of nowhere, that adoption fell through. Our baby would be going to another home. *Our* baby. I was devastated and confused, my eyes blinded by tears of grief and disappointment. Months went by, and still, no matter how hard I prayed, the longing in my heart to love another child would not leave. I couldn't understand why God put this dream in my heart when it only led to loss.

Then one Sunday I was in my office at church preparing for a service when one of our childcare workers knocked on my door. She was upset. A little boy in an elementary classroom was pulling down his pants and showing off his genitals. I told her to bring him to my office immediately. As I waited for him, I planned the lecture I was about to give this naughty boy.

Five minutes later the most adorable little five-year-old walked into my office. He was so small, his big, sad brown eyes barely able to peer over my desktop. Was this the naughty boy? Surely not. As he climbed up onto my lap and laid his head on my shoulder, my eyes began to water. I could sense that something wasn't right, and God was whispering to my heart, *Debbie, I am about to open your eyes to my will.*

Making some inquiries, I learned the little boy's name was Timmy. He had been rescued in the middle of the night from a severely abusive situation and was now safe in the home of a foster family in our church. Later we learned that his was considered one of the worst cases of abuse in the history of our county. He had basically been tortured.

I cried all the way home. I was trying to understand what God was speaking to my heart, but honestly, I was certain that he wanted us to adopt Timmy.

When John walked in the door, I had my speech ready. I was going to convince him that God had finally answered our prayers for a fourth child. I stood tall and confident as I told him what had happened and how I thought Timmy was the answer to our prayers.

John said something I will never forget. I knew God was speaking through him. "Debbie, could it be that you're being called to rescue thousands of children but all you can see is the one? Is it possible that your faith is too small and that God has a bigger plan than yours?"

He was right. God had been trying to get my attention for a long time. He wanted me to see past my will to his. And with that realization, I went to work. Within weeks, and with the help of wonderful people in our church, Timmy was in the process of being adopted. And a year later, through our church, I launched Cherish Kids, a ministry to children who need a place to call home. Throughout the ten years this ministry has been at work, it has helped to connect thousands of children to families through foster and adoption support.

It took a long time for me to see that God had a bigger plan in mind, that he was going to use my heartache and disappointment in ways I couldn't imagine.

Have you ever wondered what God's will is? Perhaps, like me, you prayed about something for a while, full of faith and belief that God wanted it to happen—only for that request to go seemingly unanswered. Or perhaps you believed you knew what God's plan was for your life and worked hard to follow his lead—only to find yourself facing a dead end. At times like these, we're left wondering what God's will is—if he changed his mind or if we got it wrong to begin with.

When God doesn't move the way we hoped, we can struggle with disappointment and despair and doubt his goodness. We can reason that our request is a good one—for the healing of a sick friend, a job opportunity to come through, an engagement ring placed on our finger, a baby conceived. But here's what I learned: often, our human will is nearsighted, our hopes and expectations limited to our finite human comprehension. God's knowledge, however, goes far beyond ours, and in the middle of our questions, discomfort, and yes, even pain, God's good plan is still at work, his kingdom and his will drawing ever nearer to our heart and life. Our expectations and dreams seem so important to us, but they don't compare to the marvelous ways God might want to use them to reveal his glory to others around us.

Keep on dreaming and hoping, because God might be planning to combine your dream and his will for a purpose far greater than you could ever imagine.

———

Surrendering our plans to God's will isn't always easy. When Jesus prayed, "Your will be done," he was speaking from a place of gracious understanding.

During your prayer time today, read what Jesus prayed to his Father in Luke 22:42. How do his words affect your thinking about surrendering to God's will? As you pray, take your hopes and dreams to him with open hands, asking him to help you trust your future to him completely.

Bringing Down Heaven

Jesus went into Galilee, where he preached God's Good News. "The time promised by God has come at last!" he announced. "The Kingdom of God is near!"

MARK 1:14–15

The overarching story of the entire Bible could be summarized with these seven words: *on earth as it is in heaven.* This theme is played out on multiple levels throughout Scripture—God giving us light and life with his breath; Jesus, the Son of God, coming to live with us and reconcile us back to God; our future hope of Jesus's eventual return to earth at the end of time.

I just love the picture of our holy, loving God stepping down into our world and our lives and his kingdom springing up in his wake. Heaven is where God is. When we pray "on earth as it is in heaven," we allow our lives to be stepping-stones for God's kingdom here on earth.

God's kingdom is coming. He is drawing nearer to redeem everything on earth. Ephesians 1:9–10 tells us, "God has now revealed to us his mysterious will regarding Christ—which is to fulfill his own good plan. And this is the plan: At the right time he will bring everything together under the authority of Christ—everything in heaven and on earth." Each one of us is like a bridge between God and this world as heaven touches earth through our faith and prayers. This happens on two levels—not just personal, but global.

I know it sounds crazy: you and I having the ability to pray down God's kingdom on a global scale! But it's the truth. God loves to partner with us! I don't know why; I just know he can do all these things through his power and in his own way. He not only invites us to join in the work of building his kingdom here on earth but also authorizes us and *gives us power* through the Holy Spirit to partner with him in his great redemptive mission. We are given the privilege and authority to make an impact on his kingdom at the global level when we pray.

All the news about political upheaval, government issues, controversies, religious tensions, wars and fighting, and death and natural disasters that constantly bombards us can be overwhelming and cause fear if we don't know what to do. But the news can also call us to prayer. When I hear it, I have to look to God for strength. I've learned that when I go to my knees in prayer and ask him to step in, to make himself known, my spirit settles with the knowledge that he hears my cry for the world.

I am both astounded and encouraged when I think of the millions of prayers for the world uttered every day. Jesus's prayer for his disciples in John 17:9–26 transcends time and space as it covers every single one of us who believe in his name. These global prayers are still at work today.

The prayers and work of God's people, of you and me through his church, penetrate darkness and usher in the will and power of God.

The prayers and work of God's people, of you and me through his church, penetrate darkness and usher in the will and power of God. In Matthew 16:19, Jesus said, "I will give you the keys of heaven's kingdom realm to forbid on earth that which is forbidden in heaven, and to release on earth that which is released in heaven" (TPT).

Your prayers are making a difference on the earth even when you can't see how. They're holding back the darkness, bringing hope to the hopeless, and opening blind eyes to the truth of the gospel. Your prayers echo across time, across space, across the physical limits of this world, and like a bridge they connect us to the extraordinary love and power of our Father God. They not only affect the here and now, but the future—the future of your children and their children.

Only two weeks after the tragedy of 9/11, John and I were flying home from a trip to New York City. We were in the middle of an overwhelmingly challenging season in the ministry. We had a massive building project that was way over budget. We were also overwhelmed with the responsibilities of leading our growing church through this horrible time in our country while we ourselves were discouraged.

As I stared out the window at the clouds, tears streamed down my face. I whispered, "God, we need your help." Then I heard him whisper these words back to me: *Debbie, the prayers your grandma Alice prayed for you are being heard by me today. I will answer them and give you the strength you need to make it through.*

My grandma Alice was an amazing person. I loved to hear her pray, and that was often. Now the words she had prayed over me countless times were heard by

God, and he was answering her prayers to bring the power of heaven to earth and my situation. In that moment, God gave me a tiny glimpse of how heaven collides with earth through prayer. This experience reminds me of Michelangelo's painting in the Sistine Chapel—God's big powerful hand reaching down from heaven to touch ours.

Like the prayers of my grandma Alice, your prayers are making a bigger difference than you realize. Your prayers are holding back darkness. Your prayers are affecting people both near to you and far from you in ways that might be revealed to you only in eternity. Your faith-filled words to God are eternal not only for the here and now but also for the days to come and for those who will need them long after you're gone. This is our hope and our mission, for one day, just as the prophet Zechariah wrote, "The LORD will be king over *all the earth*. On that day there will be one LORD—his name alone will be worshiped" (Zechariah 14:9, emphasis mine).

Your prayers are powerful! With every prayer you pray, you make way for God's kingdom to touch the lives of people, communities, governments, and nations on earth, his power moving through your prayers now and into eternity.

Reflect on what the words *on earth as it is in heaven* mean to you personally. When you think of your prayers expanding the influence of God's kingdom on earth, will that thought affect how you pray for your family, your friends, your school, your workplace—even your church? In your journal or in the space provided, make a list of the ways you want to personally and purposefully bring heaven to earth through your prayers.

Surprise Trash

Every good gift and every perfect gift is from above, coming down from the Father of lights.

JAMES 1:17 ESV

John and I married when we were nineteen years old, and when we did, we were poor by every standard—except love. We had a lot of that but little else.

Our first home the summer we were married was the chicken coop behind his parents' farmhouse. And no, I am not making this up. His mom and dad had renovated the little barn into a tiny two-bedroom house. I thought it was perfect. We furnished it with a rocking chair, a bed, a lime-green love seat, two chairs, and a grandfather clock that my grandpa had given to us as a wedding gift. That was pretty much it.

Our chicken coop/house was just the beginning of a journey of trusting in God's provision and of seeing him provide for us over and over. One of the most memorable answers to prayer came from a heap of trash. Our first baby, David, was just six months old when we packed up our few belongings to move from Springfield, Missouri, to Kansas. We had accepted the invitation to be the lead pastors of a church in the small town of Colby. On the way, we stopped at a little hotel to spend the night, and there, just outside of Topeka, a pregnancy test revealed that David was going to be a brother.

Right there on the bathroom floor, God and I had a conversation about timing. I cried . . . and so did David! I worried how we were going to handle and provide for two babies, adjust to a new home, and manage the responsibilities of pastoring. We were just twenty-one years old.

I remember unloading our belongings once we arrived and wondering how we would afford a second crib, diapers, and everything else needed to make our new house a home—like a dresser for our clothes, which were piled in boxes on the floor.

I decided to start praying, and I also decided to get practical and particular in my praying: "God, we need a dresser. Please find us one."

Days later, John walked through the back door of our tiny kitchen shouting, "Debbie! You'll never guess what I found!" He held up what looked like just a plain, unexciting piece of unfinished wood. "The rest is in the truck!"

"The rest of what?" I questioned, unimpressed with what he was showing me.

"The rest of the dresser. I found it at the dump, and, Debbie, isn't it beautiful?"

John had been cleaning out the basement of the church. He'd taken a truckload of trash to the city dump, and there in the rubble he spied God's provision and answer to my prayer. The dresser was in pieces, but with a few screws and a fresh coat of varnish, it looked like new. It was a gorgeous piece of furniture—solid oak with beautiful, ornate detailing.

When I looked at it, I couldn't stop smiling—and crying! It wasn't just that God had answered my prayer. The dresser was *better and more beautiful* than any dresser I could have dreamed up. To top things off, it perfectly matched the antique bed I had purchased before we were married. How incredible is that!

Our heavenly Father loves to take care of our needs. He has provided for John and me over and over when we've asked for his help. Starting a life together in ministry was financially challenging, but every time we had a need, God was there. Bags of groceries appeared on our front steps when we were out of food—more than once! When our three kids were all under three years old, we would find bags of disposable diapers sitting in our car every Sunday after church. To this day I don't know where they came from, but they were like diaper manna from heaven! Surprise checks showed up in the mail just in time to cover an outstanding bill. An air conditioner for our sweltering little house, a brand-new lawn mower showing up in our driveway, and yes, a miracle dresser from a trash heap (which, by the way, I will never part with because it still makes me smile)—the list goes on and on and on.

I love what Jesus says in Matthew 7:9–11, and I think the Passion Translation of the Bible words it well: "Do you know of any parent who would give his hungry child, who asked for food, a plate of rocks instead? Or when asked for a piece of fish, what parent would offer his child a snake instead? If you, imperfect as you are, know how to lovingly take care of your children and give them what's best, how much more ready is your heavenly Father to give wonderful gifts to those who ask him?"

Our heavenly Father is a good dad. He loves to pour out gifts, resources, and treasures on his children. All we need to do is ask. We can have the confidence not only that God will take care of our needs but that he's waiting and willing to do so.

When we ask God to give us our daily bread, we're asking him to meet our needs *when we need them.* And that's usually how he prefers to work. Maybe he won't provide when we expect him to, but his provision is always on time and perfect. Dietrich Bonhoeffer, a German pastor and theologian, once wrote, "We are privileged to know that he knows our needs before we ask him. This is what gives Christian prayer its boundless confidence and its joyous certainty. It matters little what form of prayer we adopt or how many words we use, what matters is the faith which lays hold on God and touches the heart of the Father who knew us long before we came to him."[1] His words are even more meaningful when you understand where Bonhoeffer was when he wrote them. He was fighting against the Nazi regime and risking his life by leading underground seminaries and churches. His needs and the needs of those relying on him must have been great, and yet what confidence he had in God's provision.

Our God is not a God of only the big things. He is a God of the details. He cares about the little daily needs that are important to you and your life—like dressers and diapers. The truth is, like children who have little understanding of all their fathers do to ensure they have what they need (food on the table, milk in the fridge, socks in the drawer—even toys to delight in), we see only a tiny glimpse of everything God is doing for us behind the scenes.

> Our God is not a God of only the big things. He is a God of the details.

Philippians 4:19 reminds us of this wonderful assurance: "My God will liberally supply (fill until full) your every need according to His riches in glory in Christ Jesus" (AMP).

When you have a specific need, your Father God wants you to look to him for help. He cares that you are nourished and that your needs are supplied, and he desires for you to enjoy every single thing he provides. And remember, sometimes his provision comes from places you might never expect. Keep your eyes open—a miracle surprise could be on the way!

What specific things do you need today? I encourage you to first remember how God has met your needs in the past and then look to him as your heavenly Father with the trust of a child for what you need.

One way to be reminded of his goodness is to create a list of the specific things you've asked him to provide, and then when the answer comes, write down how and when. Then when you are a grandma like me, you can tell your grandkids the stories of how God showed up and took care of you!

He Did So You Can

**Since we are now joined to Christ, we have been
given the treasures of redemption by his blood—
the total cancellation of our sins—all because of the
cascading riches of his grace.**

EPHESIANS 1:7 TPT

Have you ever had your heart broken? I'm pretty sure I
know the answer to that!

We humans are surrounded by other humans, and news
flash, none of us are perfect. We all struggle to keep our
selfish and sinful nature in check. So I'm fairly certain
that at some point you experienced the pain of hurtful
words, unkindness, mistreatment, or even betrayal by

someone you thought you could trust completely. And that afterward, you were left in a puddle of hurt and anger, your heart feeling as though it had broken into a thousand pieces.

I know. I've been there.

Whether the pain is great or little, if you don't deal with the hurt caused by someone in your life it can grow into bitterness, damaging your spirit and straining your relationship with God. Forgiving those who have hurt you is one of the most important and necessary acts of love you will ever choose to do. Andrew Murray put it this way: "As bread is the first need of the body, so forgiveness for the soul. And the provision for the one is as sure as for the other. We are children, but sinners too."[1]

The heart posture of someone who refuses to forgive or ask for forgiveness is one of entitlement. It's true that as believers of Jesus, we are God's children and heirs. Our worth is priceless. But Jesus consistently taught his followers to expect mistreatment. He instructed them to turn the other cheek when they were treated unfairly, to forgive even if the offender doesn't ask for it, and to look over an offense. Why? Because that's what Christ did for us.

Romans 5:8 says, "God shows his love for us in that while we were still sinners, Christ died for us" (ESV).

What an incredible statement. God didn't wait for the murderer, the sex offender, the thief, the abusive or unfaithful spouse, the betraying follower, or for any one of us to repent or ask him for help before Christ laid down his life and paid for our sins. God opened a way into complete forgiveness even before we believed in him. While we lived in the muck of our sin, ignoring God's unconditional love for us, he gave Christ's life for us. What deep, unselfish, extravagant love!

How unfair is it, then, if we turn to someone who has hurt us—most likely in lesser ways than what Christ suffered prior to this death—and withhold the forgiveness that was given to us freely? As Colossians 3:13 says, "Make allowance for each other's faults, and forgive anyone who offends you. Remember, the Lord forgave you, so you must forgive others." In our self-centered human condition, it's easy to feel we are more perfect and more deserving than we really are. But we've all hurt someone, either intentionally or accidentally. And unfortunately, unless we go live in a cave all alone, we will most likely do it again before Jesus returns. That is not an excuse; it's fact. Although redeemed, we still live in earthen vessels that need God's grace to cover our selfish imperfections. So although we've all surely been hurt by the faults and flaws of others, we must not lose sight of our own imperfections.

Now, I'm not saying this is easy. It can be difficult for us to let go of the hurt and pain caused by the words and actions of other people, especially those we love. Sometimes it seems the offense is so great that it's altogether impossible to forgive. But the bottom line is this: holding on to an offense and withholding forgiveness is deadly to our spirits. It's sinful. And if left unchecked, it will eventually create a wall between us and God. That's why we want to keep our hearts free from bitterness, and the only way to do that is to surrender our hurt and pain to God and then choose to forgive.

Not too long ago I met Janie, a young woman who started coming to our church. She opened up to me and shared her story. When she was just ten years old, her mother began to traffic her for sex to men in their community so she could have money for drugs. For nearly seven years, until she found a way out, Janie was severely abused sexually, physically, and emotionally. Though the sexual and physical abuse stopped once Janie escaped, her mom continued to remind her every day that she was worthless and unloved. The abuse and terrible words from the one person she should have been able to trust cut deep into her heart and mind. She believed them to be true, and over and over she tried to end her "worthless" life. Yet somehow she never succeeded.

One day she was invited to attend the Designed for Life Women's Conference at our church, and there, for the first time ever, she heard about a man named Jesus who loved her completely and unconditionally. He didn't view her as worthless but as beautifully created on purpose and for a purpose. God didn't love her because of anything she had done for him; he loved her just because of who she was—a girl designed by God and worthy of his love. She learned that Jesus died to rescue her from spiritual hell and that by believing in him, she could find freedom from her past and healing for the pain of rejection and abuse. Right then and there, she made the decision to commit her heart to him, and her life was transformed.

Through encouragement, prayer, and the example of Jesus, Janie discovered the freedom to forgive her mother. It hasn't been easy or simple, but with the support of her new church family, Janie has built strong boundaries to protect herself from the individuals who hurt her. It's important to know that forgiveness doesn't equal trusting those who have hurt you. Forgiveness doesn't even mean you have to have relationships with the people you've forgiven. Sometimes that's not possible or even good. Forgiveness is a matter of your heart, not anyone else's. It's trusting that *God* will take care of whatever is needed in the hearts of those who hurt you.

As Janie opened her wounded soul to Jesus and began the task of working through her anger and pain, she was astounded by Christ's fierce love for her and how his love filled her heart to love and forgive even those who had hurt her. Her choice to forgive freed her to begin growing into the strong, beautiful woman of God she was designed to be.

Today Janie is a new person, an active ministry leader who serves to help others find the same love and freedom in Christ that she did.

Maybe you need to seek forgiveness from someone. Maybe, like Janie, you need to extend forgiveness to someone who has hurt you. But you don't have to do this in your own power. When Christ paid for every sin, the cost included our sin of unforgiveness. He works in us, helping us to forgive others because he first forgave us.

Let me say this: in my experience, forgiveness is not a one-time act. Years ago, John and I were betrayed by someone we had been friends with for twenty years. We were deeply hurt. But by God's grace we made the decision to forgive. That choice didn't mean our feelings of hurt were wiped away. It didn't mean that when we saw that person, we jumped up and down in excitement. No, the memories and feelings welled back up in our hearts, so we had to choose again and again to forgive until finally the choice of forgiveness covered the pain and replaced it with love.

The more time we spend with God in prayer, the more we become like Jesus. And the more we become like Jesus, the more capacity we have to forgive and love others like he does. As Paul said in Ephesians 4:32, "Be kind and affectionate toward one another. Has God graciously forgiven you? Then graciously forgive one another in the depths of Christ's love" (TPT).

> **The more time we spend with God in prayer, the more we become like Jesus.**

One of my faith heroes, Holocaust survivor Corrie ten Boom, said, "Forgiveness is an act of the will, and the will can function regardless of the temperature of the heart."[2]

Do you need to extend forgiveness to someone? I encourage you not to wait until you feel like forgiving and not to base your decision to forgive on how you think the other person will respond. As you choose to love like Jesus did, God will soften your heart and give you the strength to love again.

Run, Girl, Run

DAY 18

The temptations in your life are no different from what others experience. And God is faithful. He will not allow the temptation to be more than you can stand. When you are tempted, he will show you a way out.

1 CORINTHIANS 10:13

We don't typically talk about temptation with our friends, but honestly, we should. It's a big deal, and it's constantly lurking around us. Satan loves to tempt us, and more than anything he wants to see us fail.

Satan hates God, and because you're a believer in Jesus Christ, he hates you. He's hell-bent on destroying you. His desire is always and forever to lead you away from what is good and right and beautiful. Since the day

Adam and Eve listened to his lies in the garden, Satan has been spewing his twisted truth to tempt every follower of God.

He is a thief, a liar, and a deceiver. The Bible says he masquerades as goodness, pretending to offer something better than what God's grace provides. He tempts us with things disguised to look right when they are wrong, safe when they are dangerous, fun and life-giving when they lead to pain and death. That is why the Word of God warns you over and over to "flee" temptation. That is why Jesus directed the disciples to pray not only against sin but also against the very seeds of sin. He knew that even the closest of his followers needed to be prepared to face the devil's bait. Temptation is tempting, and to avoid it we need to be ready.

If we could retrace the steps of a girl who finds herself struggling with sin, we would see that she's been through a gradual process. It doesn't happen all at once. It's a step-by-step backing away from the presence of God and the practices that strengthen our faith and commitment to him. We stop going to church and surrounding ourselves with other believers. We start filling our minds with things we know we shouldn't. Our Bibles are left on the shelf. Little by little, we drift farther and farther away from the presence of God. And the farther we get from God's presence, the more susceptible we are to the whispers of temptation. We begin to lose perspective on what's true and good, and we become vulnerable to the lies of the Enemy.

Every girl who has committed to following Jesus has been tempted to sin. James 1:14 puts it this way: "Each one is tempted when he is dragged away, enticed and baited [to commit sin] by his own [worldly] desire" (AMP). I have experienced temptation many, many times. As a young girl, I was tempted to drink and party with my peers. Before John and I were married, I was tempted to compromise my convictions and have sex. As a young mom, surrounded by diapers and crying babies, I was tempted to fill my mind with things that were more exciting than everyday life. During times of discouragement, I've been tempted to quit. Satan has used his lies to discourage me from writing these very words to you, tempting me to doubt that God was with me. The battle was real and hard. I almost quit.

Temptation is temptation because it's tempting. But temptation is not sin; it's the bait. As my dad would say, "You can't keep the birds from flying over your head, but you can keep them from building a nest in your hair." In other words, we all will be tempted, but we don't have to give in.

So how do you flee temptation? Pray and run. That's it. It's that simple. Pray and run, girlfriend!

When you find yourself struggling with temptation, the best thing you can do is get on your knees and spend time in God's presence, asking him to help you be strong. Jesus said, "Pray, so that you will not give in to temptation" (Matthew 26:41). Prayer strengthens your resolve to stand strong against Satan's lies. Prayer gives you a clear mind. It empowers you to recognize Satan's lies and equips you with strength to win the battle against temptation and sin. Prayer gives you the power to run.

> Prayer gives you a clear mind. It empowers you to recognize Satan's lies and equips you with strength to win the battle against temptation and sin.

So, dear girl, let's get personal for a minute.

If your marriage is in a season of challenge (yes, we all have them), you need to run from the guy who causes you to think compromising thoughts (and you know what I mean—don't go looking for him on social media!).

If your friend invites you to drink and party with her, just say no. Who knows, your commitment to do what's right and guard your heart might encourage her to run too.

If you and your boyfriend are struggling to keep your hands off each other, don't hang out alone in dark, secluded places. And if your boyfriend is pressuring you to have sex, please, run from *him*. You deserve better!

If you struggle to take care of your body and your health, start running past the aisles with the chips, soda, and Oreos and quit filling your house with junk food. I get it. I used to drink a Coke a day and eat French fries as if I needed them to survive. You can do it!

If you struggle with overspending to soothe your emotions or you hide purchases from those you should be accountable to, run and find scissors to cut up your credit cards.

The struggle is real, but the truth is that fleeing from temptation isn't complicated. It just takes guts and a commitment to choose the way out God provides for us. And we can. You can. Why? Because through his power in you, you have the power to resist every temptation Satan tries to entice you with.

First Corinthians 10:13 says, "The temptations in your life are no different from what others experience. And God is faithful. He will not allow the temptation to be more than you can stand. When you are tempted, he will show you a way out so that you can endure." We do not fight this battle alone. God, who is far greater than Satan, is fighting with us and for us. And prayer is our powerful weapon. When you draw near to God's holy and loving presence, he's there to hold you up and help you stand.

Now, I don't want you to be surprised if in the middle of this prayer journey, when you're intentionally seeking to spend more time with God, the temptation to doubt him feels the strongest. When Jesus went into the wilderness for forty days to fast and pray, he experienced the most intense temptations from Satan. Even Jesus, as close as he was to the Father, battled temptation. Hebrews 4:15–16 says this about him: "This High Priest of ours understands our weaknesses, for he faced all of the same testings we do, yet he did not sin. So let us come boldly to the throne of our gracious God. There we will receive his mercy, and we will find grace to help us when we need it most."

God understands your weaknesses, your struggles, and your temptations to give in to sin. And as you look to him for help, as you spend time in his presence, he is going to help you run, girl, run!

If you're struggling with temptation and feel like you don't have the strength to run, you're not alone in this battle. As you look to God in prayer and take time to be in his Word, he will help you to be strong. I encourage you to read Ephesians 6:12–17 in the New Living

Translation and consider how the words strengthen your resolve to stand against temptation.

Perhaps you would say to me, "Debbie, I lost the battle with temptation, and now I'm living in sin." But your heavenly Father still loves you, dear girl. He has not abandoned you. His grace is greater than your sin. And in a heartbeat, he will welcome you back into his arms when you come running to him with a repentant heart.

Deliver Us

Not even the powers of hell can separate us from God's love.

ROMANS 8:38

In the summer of 1990, John and I felt God leading us to Kansas City to start a new church. It was a huge leap of faith to leave a place of ministry we loved and move our three little preschoolers to a city where we knew not one other person. As soon as we had moved into our little duplex, we began inviting people to be a part of the church that would launch in the fall of that year.

We sensed it was a spiritual battle from the start. Despite thousands (and I mean thousands!) of phone calls and personal door-to-door invitations, on our first

Sunday a total of three people were interested enough in the church to visit. After a year of doing everything we could think to do, we grew to thirteen people, and five of them were our family! Financially, we were in a challenging situation, and the pressure to keep our little church moving forward was putting a great deal of stress on our marriage. John and I were both struggling with discouragement. It was obvious that Satan was trying his best to take advantage of our emotional exhaustion, because we were beginning to believe his lies: *You aren't good enough. You are a failure. You need to quit.*

And then this happened one night.

It was after midnight. John and I were lying in bed, and once again I was struggling to sleep. Suddenly, the atmosphere in the room changed, and I felt the presence of evil. It was terrifying. I froze in fear as my heart began to beat as if it were going to come out of my chest. I had sensed evil before, but this was different. It was in our bedroom! With what little voice I could muster, and without moving a muscle, I said John's name, hoping he was still awake. He whispered back immediately, "I know. I feel it too."

There in the darkness, we rolled toward each other, held hands, and began to pray and speak the Word of God out loud, lifting our voices to him in confident and bold prayer. For the next two hours, we prayed together, claiming the blood of Jesus over our home and commanding the evil spirit to leave in Jesus's name. And it did. It had to. Sometime around two in the morning, we both felt the darkness leave, and we soon fell asleep with God's presence and power surrounding us.

We are in a battle, my friend—a spiritual battle of cosmic proportions. Just look around you. Turn on the news. Evil is real and present in our world. Sin is rampant, and Satan is on the rampage, waging a war against all that is good and right.

In the world where we live, popular media, music, and movies have made Satan out to be a superhero, highlighting and promoting his evil agenda to a degree that has never been seen before. Unfortunately, many Christians don't realize the danger in opening up their hearts and minds to this messaging. I see it all the time. In the "innocent watching" of movies, they allow the Enemy to deteriorate their faith. Remember, he's out to entice people to sin and go against God's laws. His primary way of attacking us is to discourage us from believing that God's Word is real, right, and true. He does it subtly at first, so that we don't even realize the seriousness of what's happening.

Don't be deceived by the lies Satan has devised to fool the culture around us. Every day in our courtrooms, our classrooms, our workplaces, and our homes the Enemy is working at what he does best: steal, kill, and destroy. He's turned right into wrong and bad into good. He's convinced society to trade God's truth for a lie: the sanctity of life, family, and marriage is under attack and no longer valued or respected. My desire for you is to be strong in the Lord, enabling you to withstand any lie he brings your way so—as 2 Corinthians 2:11 says—"we would not be outwitted by Satan; for we are not ignorant of his designs" (ESV).

Sometimes, to get our attention and remind us that there is a battle raging in the spirit world between darkness and light, God allows the spiritual veil around us to be pulled back. The apostle Paul explained it this way: "We are not fighting against flesh-and-blood enemies, but against evil rulers and authorities of the unseen world, against mighty powers in this dark world, and against evil spirits in the heavenly places" (Ephesians 6:12). Satan and his demons are real and actively prowling around, trying to steal, kill, and destroy all who are willing to stand for the truth and righteousness. Paul wanted to remind believers of that fact. Why? So they wouldn't be surprised when they faced a battle.

The spiritual battle we fought that night in our bedroom is forever etched in my mind. I remember vividly how fear was our initial reaction to the power of evil we felt, but as John and I began to pray and voice our trust in God's power to deliver us, our fear turned to faith. Jesus said this in 1 John 4:4: "You belong to God, my dear children. You have already won a victory . . . because the Spirit who lives in you is greater than the spirit who lives in the world." When we pray to God for his help and speak the name of Jesus, Satan has no choice but to flee!

This is what we have to remember first and foremost: "Prayer is not a preparation for the battle; it is the battle!"[1] Prayer is a battle we're fighting for our homes, our communities, and our nations. As believers in Jesus Christ, we are soldiers in the army of God, and Satan and his demons are fighting against us on the other side. We know Jesus conquered evil when he gave his life on the cross and that he triumphed over death itself when he rose again. That is why praying in God's name is so powerful—it's our weapon and our protection against the Enemy. Remember the words in Ephesians 6:16: "Above all, lift up the [protective] shield of faith with which you can extinguish all the flaming arrows of the evil one" (AMP). Those words are a reminder to us that Satan is always shooting "arrows" at us from every direction. But if we're prepared, ready to put our faith in action through prayer, he's the one who should be afraid.

> **Praying in God's name is so powerful—it's our weapon and our protection against the Enemy.**

When the Christians in Ephesus, the people to whom Paul was writing, were facing spiritual oppression, he reminded them to "be strong in the Lord and in his mighty power" (Ephesians 6:10). Then in Ephesians 6:10–20, he gave them a game plan for praying for God's power to fight. First, like a soldier getting ready for battle, he said to put on the armor of God—every piece. We need it all to fight with a commitment to truth, righteousness, and peace that comes from the good news of the gospel, along with faith, salvation, and the Word of God.

Second, in verse 18 Paul told them to "pray in the Spirit at all times and on every occasion." What does that look like? As believers, we have access to praying "in the Spirit." When we don't know how to pray or even what to say, the Holy Spirit, who lives inside of us, prays for us. Isn't this awesome? The Holy Spirit is a powerful resource when we're in the middle of a spiritual battle.

Finally, Paul said to stay alert, to pay attention! Earlier, we talked about how slippery and subtle Satan's lies can be. We stay alert to his lies by being "persistent in [our] prayers, for *all* believers everywhere" (verse 18, emphasis mine). To borrow the metaphor of the soldier again, as fellow Christians we're called to watch one another's backs. Through prayer, we battle the Enemy's attacks against our brothers and our sisters around the world.

What a powerful army we get to be a part of! Guarded with God's victory, we're alert and ready to fight, standing shoulder to shoulder, praying for one another. And with Jesus leading the way, we never need to be afraid. We just need to stand firm with our weapon of prayer and shield of faith!

During your time in prayer today, read through Ephesians 6:10–20. Underline it and turn it into a personal prayer of protection for yourself, your family, your community, and your nation. Make a list of people you want to pray for regularly, and then pray for one person each day and message them to let them know you did.

SHE PRAYS
Trust

WITH

PART THREE

This One Thing

Pour out all your worries and stress upon him *and leave them there*, for he always tenderly cares for you.

1 PETER 5:7 TPT

When you purpose to pray, do you ever find your mind wandering to the next thing on your to-do list or to that text that popped up on your phone? Do you catch yourself thinking about the dishes in the sink, the emails in your in-box, your kid's school project, that Instagram post, or how you need to finish a task? Do you sometimes feel pressure to forgo your quiet time with God altogether, because even though you know you need him more than ever, you just don't seem to have time to spare?

I know that feeling . . . today! I'm under a deadline, and I'm being tempted right now to do the work of writing instead of what will help me most—time in God's presence. So I'm leaving you for now. . . .

I'm back. Nothing is more life-giving, refreshing, and faith-building than being with Jesus and taking time to worship him and rest in his love. Yet it's so easy to let pulls of lesser importance steal the gift of sitting still and receiving from him.

I get that, and so did a girl in the Bible named Martha.

Martha was probably a perfectionist, preferring everything in order. She most likely would have loved sticky notes. Getting things done and checked off her list probably made her feel good about herself.

One day Jesus showed up at her house with some of his men, and she wanted nothing more than to impress him with how hard she could work for him. Her heart was in the right place—at least she thought so. Wasn't that what Jesus would expect from a good and godly girl?

I've read this story about Martha and her sister, Mary, many times, but until I read it again this week, I didn't see or understand how connected it is to prayer. It comes right before Jesus's teaching to the disciples on the Lord's Prayer, right before one of the disciples asked him to teach them how to pray.

Jesus and his crew of disciples were headed toward Jerusalem, and along the way they stopped at Mary and Martha's house for a visit and to get some rest. Maybe you remember these two girls. They were the sisters of Lazarus, whom Jesus had raised from the dead.

Thirteen tired and hungry men showed up, and it was the two women's job to feed them all. So as their guests were resting their tired feet, Martha headed to the kitchen. As she did, Mary sat herself down, right at Jesus's feet.

I can just picture Martha saying, "Mary, I'm going to need your help" in a matter-of-fact, follow-me tone, and then my "do everything right" friend making a to-do list in her head as she scurries into the kitchen, wiping beads of sweat from her forehead: *get the bread dough mixed and rising, make stew . . .*

An hour later, the dough is rising, the lamb-and-lentil stew is bubbling in a pot, the hors d'oeuvres are ready to be plated—and there is still a lot to do. The table needs to be set, the brownie batter mixed . . .

Where is Mary? What in the world is that girl doing? Didn't her sister understand how important this dinner was? They were feeding Jesus!

I can also picture her peeking into the living room and seeing Mary sitting right where she'd left her an hour earlier.

That's it! I've had it!

Right then and there, the pressure to get it all done and do everything right comes boiling to the surface. And with that, Martha marches to Jesus with her hands waving in the air. "Lord," she says, "doesn't it seem unfair to you that my sister just sits here while I do all the work? Tell her to come and help me" (Luke 10:40).

Okay, I'm laughing out loud right now. This is a hilarious moment in the Bible!

I can so relate to Martha. Can't you? The demands of life seem to be piling up, and you want to go to Jesus and complain because you're absolutely positive he'll understand and even help you accomplish all the tasks pressing in on you. And anyone watching will see how good you are at doing everything perfectly.

Ouch!

Now listen to how Jesus responds to her: "My dear Martha, you are worried and upset over all these details! There is only one thing worth being concerned about. Mary has discovered it, and it will not be taken away from her" (Luke 10:41–42).

With just a few words, Jesus beautifully contrasts the hearts of the two women. Mary was focused on being with Jesus. She wasn't afraid to go against the cultural norms that dictated women had to work to serve the men rather than take a place at the table and contribute to the conversation. She understood that the most important thing for her to do wasn't to worry about being liked or noticed, missing all the activity around her. The most important thing was to be close to Jesus.

Martha wasn't a bad girl; she wanted to do what was right. Her work was important for the comfort and well-being of those around her. People have to eat, right? But she was caught up in what was expected of her, in numerous tasks that demanded her time and energy. And she completely missed the point. Martha allowed her own expectation—doing everything "perfectly"—to dictate her priorities, all under the guise of serving Jesus. But he had come to be *with* her, and her lack of spiritual awareness and of what she personally needed from him caused her to be frustrated with everything around her.

Martha didn't have peace because of this one thing: she was spiritually anemic. She needed to take some time at the feet of Jesus. As Psalm 16:8–9 says, "I have set the LORD continually before me; because He is at my right hand, I will not be shaken. Therefore my heart is glad and my glory [my innermost self] rejoices; my body too will dwell [confidently] in safety" (AMP).

We've all been there with the pressure to be it all, do it all, look good, plan perfectly, be at the top of our game, Instagram five times a day, manicure our eyebrows—and on top of all that, maintain a Pinterest-worthy house. That kind of pressure is crushing. I can relate. Even though I love time alone with God and I know it's the most important thing I could give my attention to, I can allow the less important to crowd out the most important.

Every season has its own unique pressures and responsibilities. They might look different for you than they do for me, but they're every bit as real. Even work that's good and God-centered activity can distract us from what we need most—spending time at the feet of Jesus. As the great church reformer Martin Luther is often credited with saying, "I have so much to do that I shall spend the first three hours in prayer,"[1] or as others have paraphrased, "I'm too busy not to pray." It sounds counterintuitive, but it's the truth.

> Prayer isn't meant to be another item on our to-do list. . . . It's our life, our hope, our strength. It's altogether the most important thing we need . . . every single day.

Prayer isn't meant to be another item on our to-do list. It's not a preliminary task to do before we can get on with our "real work." It's our life, our hope, our strength. It's altogether the most important thing we need . . . every single day.

Taking time to pray, stepping away from those mounting pressures to sit in God's presence, changes you. It renews your energy and strengthens your faith and confidence in who God is. It reframes your perspective so that rather than focusing on a mile-long to-do list, you'll see gifts and opportunities for God to show up.

Use the next page or grab your phone and make two lists, side by side if you can. On the left side, list everything that's grabbing your attention and energy—your to-do list. Whenever I do this, it quickly becomes apparent why I'm tired or stressed. We women carry a lot on our plates!

On the right side, recast each item as the gift or opportunity it is from God. As you go down the list, pray about each item, asking God for his help, energy, and peace, as well as his wisdom to know how to steward each opportunity well and focus on what's important.

Your lists might look something like this:

My to-do list:

- Pitch a new idea to my boss

- Talk to my child about
  _____

- Create a post for social media

- Finish the laundry and dishes

God's opportunity list:

- Use the gifts God has given me to inspire others

- Take this opportunity to disciple my precious child

- Be a godly influence

- Be a good steward of what God has given me

_____

_____

_____

_____

_____

_____

_____

_____

_____

I Hear you

When you call, the LORD will answer.
  "Yes, I am here," he will quickly reply.

ISAIAH 58:9

John and I have five grandsons and three granddaughters. We adore every one of them, and we love spending time with them whenever we can.

When all of them are at our house . . . my goodness, does it get wild! There are toys everywhere, the pitter-patter of little feet running around, shouts of "Don't run!" and squeals of laughter, and a thousand simultaneous conversations taking place. But crazy as it might sound, even in the midst of all that happy chaos I can pick out the voice of every single grandchild. I know each one of their voices. I bet the same is true for you and the ones you love.

Every single person has a unique sound signature to their voice. Your voice is like your thumbprint. No other person on the planet has a voice exactly like yours. The shape of your vocal cords, the size of your body, your distinct accent, the places and dialects you've been exposed to, and your personality all come together to create your one-of-a-kind voice. At this writing, 7.7 billion different voices are on this earth, and just think, God can decipher all of them. That means he knows exactly what your voice sounds like. How amazing is that?

When our daughter, Savannah, was four years old, John and I took her and her two older brothers to an amusement park. We thought it was going to be a wonderful way to spend a Saturday afternoon—and apparently, so did a lot of other people. The place was packed! We hadn't been there for more than a couple of hours when we heard a child crying for her mom and dad in the crowd behind us. John and I turned to each other in shock and fear. Without looking down to count our kids, we knew it was Savannah's cry. Somehow, as we were making our way through the crowd, she'd become separated from us. Thankfully, she was born with the mother of all cries, and we knew it well. Even in the crowd, we knew that voice belonged to our baby girl.

Like an attentive parent's, God's ear is always tuned to hear you. The moment you start talking or crying out to him, he takes notice and leans in to listen and respond to what you need. First Peter 3:12 says, "The eyes of the Lord are on the righteous, and his ears are open to their prayer" (ESV). Those words are talking about you. Remember, you are his righteous and dearly loved daughter, so anytime you speak a word or cry out to him, his attention is laser-focused on you.

Your heavenly Father has a voice, too, one meant to be easily recognizable to you.

In John 10:3–4, Jesus taught his followers how to hear God's voice by using the illustration of a shepherd and his sheep. He said, "He [God] calls his own sheep [you and me] by name and leads them out. . . . They follow him because they know his voice."

This might seem like a strange metaphor to you, but in Jesus's day, people saw shepherds caring for their flocks every day. They would have readily understood what Jesus was talking about. You see, a shepherd was with his sheep 24/7, *all day and all night long*. He never left them. And because he knew his sheep could easily become confused and frightened, he was constantly talking to them, speaking words to guide them, keep them from harm, and comfort them with his calming and reassuring voice.

Let's pause on that thought a minute. God is with you all the time, speaking to your heart through the Holy Spirit. He is constantly there to guide you, comfort you, and keep you going in the right direction. And the more you practice listening for his voice, the more you recognize it. The question is not whether God talks to you. The question is this: *When* he does, are you listening?

Hearing the voice of God is meant to be simple. The way we learn to recognize it is by tuning our hearts to listen for him. We should be so accustomed to the sound of his voice that it becomes the easiest voice for us to hear.

I'm sure right now you're thinking, *That sounds great, Debbie. But how? How does God speak, and how do I know it's him?* I want to share some ways God's voice can be heard.

Through his written Word. God has given us a special revelation of himself through Scripture. Hebrews 4:12 says, "The word of God is alive and powerful. . . . It exposes our innermost thoughts and desires." Do you want to know what God is saying and what his voice sounds like? There's no better place to begin than in the Bible! Psalm 119:105 says, "Your word is a lamp to guide my feet and a light for my path." When I'm reading God's Word each day, one of the questions I ask him is, *What do you want to say to me from your Word?*

Through his spoken word. God has always used people to speak to his children. In the Old Testament accounts, he used the prophets. In the New Testament accounts, he spoke through Jesus and the apostles. Today, by his Holy Spirit, God uses everyday people to reveal his truth to us. Whether in a powerful message from a pastor or in a casual conversation with a godly friend, God can and does speak to us through other people. Now, this doesn't mean everything said to us is from God. And if it doesn't line up with his written Word, it's for sure not from him.

Through his whispered word. God can speak any way he wants, but it seems to me that one of his favorite ways to speak is with a quiet whisper. We would love to have God speak to us in a clear and audible voice, but 99.9 percent of the time, he seems to speak to his children through a still, small whisper deep within our hearts (1 Kings 19:11–13).

I want to talk about this because I think it's really important for you to understand it and put listening for God's voice into practice. Listening to his voice is often like hearing a clear and distinct thought, one you sense is from him. It's the whisper of the Holy Spirit, telling you to do something that might even be unexpected—like *Go talk to that girl and invite her to church*, or *Text and encourage [so and so] with this Bible verse*; or even *Don't worry, sweet girl. I'm right beside you.* God's words to us aren't complicated or confusing or bizarre, my friend. He always makes sense. And his whisper always aligns us with his Word and reveals his will.

I tell this story about God's gentle whisper in my book *She Believes*:

> A couple years ago, I was in a checkout line at the grocery store one morning. In front of me was a mother with her two young children. I thought she looked tired and stressed as she set her single purchase on the conveyor belt—a dozen confetti-sprinkled cupcakes from the bakery. As I watched her digging in her purse for her wallet, I heard a whisper. *Debbie, I want you to pay for those cupcakes.*
>
> I remember thinking, *God, is that really you? I'm sure she can probably manage to pay for her own cupcakes. And besides, what if it embarrasses or upsets her?*[1]

It took just a moment for me to make my decision, and I'm so glad I decided to obey the voice of the Holy Spirit that day. More than a year later, that precious mommy sent me a beautiful note that told her side of the story. You see, she had no money in her bank account when she walked into that grocery store that morning, but she wanted to get the cupcakes for her daughter's birthday party at school. She asked God what to do, and she heard him speak: *I want you to go ahead and stop at the store and pick up cupcakes.* She had obeyed and trusted the voice of the Lord, and she wanted to share with me what happened to her family as a result:

> Since that day in the grocery store, our lives have changed and our finances have completely turned around. I am eternally grateful that you listened to God that morning. You were an angel sent by him to help place our family on the path that he has laid out before us—to trust him always and completely with everything![2]

Wow! I'm so thankful that I listened and obeyed what I heard God speak to me that day. In that moment I'd had no idea everything my $3 gift was going to do for her and her family.

Hearing from God isn't mysterious; it's personal. If you walk close to him, you will hear him speaking to you.

The quiet voice of the Holy Spirit goes with us wherever we go. He can speak to us in any situation. Like all good things, hearing God's voice takes prayer and practice. And the more we learn to train our ear to his voice in prayer, the clearer and more distinct his voice becomes. Hearing from God isn't mysterious; it's personal. If you walk close to him, you will hear him speaking to you.

I want to encourage you to make a habit of expecting God to speak to you. As you hear his voice through your Bible reading, the teaching you receive at your church and share in your small group, and the whisper of the Holy Spirit, he will lead you places you never dreamed you would go and open doors for you to bless others in unexpected ways—maybe even with a dozen cupcakes.

1, 2, 3... Rest

DAY 22

Because I, your GOD,
    have a firm grip on you and I'm not letting go.
I'm telling you, "Don't panic.
    I'm right here to help you."

ISAIAH 41:13 MSG

Anxiety is "a feeling of worry, nervousness, or unease, typically about an imminent event or something with an uncertain outcome."[1] More than twenty million women battle anxiety, persistent worry, and fear about everyday situations.[2] Anxiety is a common issue, and if this hits home for you, my friend, I hope it's comforting to know you're not alone.

We have all experienced some level of anxiety—and probably more than once. It frequently travels alongside trial and heartache and rises with unexpected disappointment or unresolvable circumstances. It can strike without warning and stick to us like unwanted glue. And if left unaddressed, anxiety and fear can warp our thinking, cripple our soul, and cause us to believe what simply is not true.

The Bible has much to say about anxious hearts. It tells us that, through the work of Christ in us, we can find victory over every—yes, every—fearful thought and worry that tries to keep us from experiencing the life God intends for us to live. And that is the truth! As daughters of our heavenly Father, you and I have a sure and solid foundation of hope and peace to stand on in every situation we face. We have every reason to trust our future to him. And by future, I mean the next minute, hour, day, week, month, year—and the forever of your life. I want you to know, without a doubt, that God has you in his hands. This day, he is watching over you, holding you, and protecting you.

Because they are just as much for you today, remember his words in Isaiah 41:8–10 to the people of Israel: "I've picked you. I haven't dropped you. Don't panic. I'm with you. There's no need to fear for I'm your God. I'll give you strength. I'll help you. I'll hold you steady, keep a firm grip on you" (MSG).

Okay, my dear, I think you might need to read those words again. Slowly. Out loud. Let the words your heavenly Father is speaking over you sink deep into your heart and mind.

If we could see ahead to what he has planned for us in the future, it would blow our minds. I love Jeremiah 29:11; it's one of my favorite go-to verses when I need a little kick in my booty, when I'm looking at tomorrow with anxious eyes, when I need to remind myself to rest in knowing that God is ahead of me, taking care of whatever concerns me: "'For I know the plans I have for you,' says the LORD. 'They are plans for good and not for disaster, to give you a future and a hope.'"

Though we can't see ahead, we can rest in the future. Why? Because our past has been set free by a merciful Savior. Because we have been given enough grace to fill an ocean. Because the well of God's love for us never runs dry. Because his peace and joy are abundant and overflowing! God has everything under control. When you look at your current circumstances through the lens of all he has done for you and all that knowing him provides, what you see should give you confidence in the middle of any situation that everything is going to be all right. You can stand on his promises, which are sure and reliable.

But it's up to you, my dear girl, to choose to trust in his promises to take care of you. Magic wands for controlling anxious thoughts don't exist. If they did, I could sell them and make a mint.

Thankfully, God has provided a way for us to experience his supernatural peace. Read Philippians 4:6–9 and look at the three practical steps found there:

1. *Purposeful Prayer.* "Don't worry about anything; instead, pray about everything" (verse 6).
2. *Purposeful Thinking.* "Fix your thoughts on what is true, and honorable, and right, and pure, and lovely, and admirable. Think about things that are excellent and worthy of praise" (verse 8).
3. *Purposeful Practice.* "Keep putting into practice all you learned and received from me [steps 1 and 2!]. . . . Then the God of peace will be with you" (verse 9).

Sometimes we spend all our time with God talking about every worry, every doubt, and every fear, leaving no time for him to wrap his loving arms around us to remind us that he is enough. Time in God's presence in quiet surrender to him is when we find the place of rest for our souls. Your heavenly Father understands fear, worry, and anxiety. He understands the depth of the emotions and thoughts you're dealing with. But he doesn't want you to build a home there. He invites you to know him more fully, trust him more deeply, and hide under the shadow of his wings.

This reminds me of my friend Kristie. One of her young sons had trouble sleeping for a while because he had horrible nightmares. At all hours of the night, he would wake up terrified, crying and shivering with a cold sweat. So Kristie began reading Psalm 91 to him just before lights out, sometimes leaving the Bible open next to his pillow so if he woke up, he would see it and be comforted by the reminder of God's constant presence. After a few nights of this, Kristie's son told her he didn't have any nightmares the nights she'd read the psalm.

> **Time in God's presence in quiet surrender to him is when we find the place of rest for our souls.**

Isn't that such a sweet reminder of how God dispels fear with his peaceful presence? When worry, fear, or anxiety threaten to overwhelm us, we can always go to God and find refuge in his presence.

I leave you with these words from Jesus: "Come to me. Get away with me and you'll recover your life. I'll show you how to take a real rest. Walk with me and work with me—watch how I do it. Learn the unforced rhythms of grace. I won't lay anything heavy or ill-fitting on you. Keep company with me and you'll learn to live freely and lightly" (Matthew 11:28–30 MSG).

I encourage you today to underline Philippians 4:6–9 in your Bible and begin to practice the simple steps found there. Then watch what God does in your heart and mind.

Distant Feeling

We come closer to God and approach him with an open heart, fully convinced by faith that nothing will keep us at a distance from him.

HEBREWS 10:22 TPT

Have you ever been in a place where God seemed distant? Where you showed up each day, read the Bible, and took time to pray, and yet it felt like he was far, far away? This sense of distance can be bewildering, frustrating, and hard to articulate and understand.

Over my thirty-five years of ministry, countless girls have shared with me their feelings of disconnect to God, struggling to understand why he doesn't seem close to them or seem to care about what they're experiencing.

I can honestly say that, even as a leader in the church, I have felt those same feelings at times. And when I look back, those moments were often connected to times of personal physical and emotional weariness.

When we're feeling God is distant, struggling to believe that he is near us when we pray, it always relates to our position, not his. Often, the distance we sense is because of our own self-doubt, a season of weak faith, or a symptom of simply forgetting our true identity in Christ. We have forgotten what Hebrews 4:16 says, that because of Jesus, we can draw near to the throne of grace, into God's very presence, with perfect confidence and assurance.

Other times, the separation we feel is just plain emotion. We're stressed with life. Our emotions are on overload and affecting our ability to think straight. Girls, let's face it. We are emotional beings! Thank goodness God understands us even when no one else can. And I have great news. Our emotions don't define the reality of who God is and his proximity to us! Just because *we* feel a distance doesn't mean his presence has left us or is far away. Deuteronomy 31:8 says, "It is the LORD who goes before you. He will be with you; he will not leave you or forsake you" (ESV).

God hasn't moved, dear one. He hasn't left your side because you're too emotional. He hasn't tired of your tears—he *made* those tears.

May I tell you what has helped me? Don't evaluate any situation at night when you're tired. Go to bed and sleep. I promise you will have a better perspective in the morning. I think that's why David said in Psalm 143:8,

> **Thank goodness God understands us even when no one else can.**

"Let the morning bring me word of your unfailing love, for I have put my trust in you" (NIV).

What I'm trying to show you is this: Feeling disconnected from God doesn't necessarily mean you've done anything wrong. You might just need to remind yourself of God's truth and then take a nap or go for a walk and refresh your mind in the sunshine.

However, sometimes that feeling of distance from God is a clue about the posture of your heart. Just like hunger or thirst tells us we need to do something to care for our physical health, so this feeling of distance is a sign that something might need to be addressed regarding your spiritual health. It might be as simple as dealing with a bad attitude, with apathy you've allowed toward the things of God, or with unforgiveness or selfishness.

The Bible tells us that when we permit sin in our life, we will feel distance. This is how the prophet Isaiah put it in Isaiah 59:1–2: "Don't think that the LORD is too weak to save you or too deaf to hear your call for help! It is because of your sins that he doesn't hear you. It is your sins that separate you from God when you try to worship him" (GNT). God's still there; you're the one who moved. Your sin caused your connection to him to weaken. As believers, nothing can separate us from his love, but our choices of disobedience can block our view of God. He's still there, graciously waiting for you to deal with your sin so that your connection to him can be restored.

God is not vindictive. He doesn't play hide-and-seek with you. He isn't calculating your mistakes and keeping track of your spiritual grade level. He is never embarrassed or ashamed of you because of your inconsistency. On the contrary, he longs to be with you even when you've messed up and failed him. And he is eagerly waiting to welcome you back into his arms just as you are. Romans 8:38–39 states it like this:

> Nothing can ever separate us from God's love. Neither death nor life, neither angels nor demons, neither our fears for today nor our worries about tomorrow—not even the powers of hell can separate us from God's love. No power in the sky above or in the earth below— indeed, nothing in all creation will ever be able to separate us from the love of God that is revealed in Christ Jesus our Lord.

Absolutely *nothing* can separate you from the love of God. That is an incredible promise! Whatever you're feeling, be sure you're connecting your feelings to the truth of God's Word. He wants you to have this confidence, that no matter what, his presence is *always* right there with you!

As you pray today, be open and honest with God about what you're feeling. Ask him to remind you that he is right there and to reveal anything that might be causing you to feel distant from him.

Then read and meditate on the words in Psalm 139:7–12 and Psalm 145:18. How do these verses remind you of God's nearness?

Worth the Wait

DAY 24

GOD proves to be good to the man who passionately
    waits,
    to the woman who diligently seeks.

LAMENTATIONS 3:25 MSG

I was searching for a specific website on my phone the
other day. But instead of the webpage, tiny little dots
popped up on the screen, forming the spinning circle of
doom. Beneath them were two simple words: "Please
wait." Ugh.

I like to think of myself as a patient person, but I'm not so
good at being still, especially if I can find a way to keep
moving. But that isn't always best. I have maneuvered
myself into some big pickles because I didn't want to wait

(expensive ones, like the kind handed to you through the car window by a person dressed in a blue uniform).

I'm one of those drivers who immediately starts looking for an alternate route when a traffic light turns yellow. For me, that's just a signal to step on the gas or find a side road to avoid the impending red light. I have a goal, and I want to keep moving.

We can find this sense of impatience in prayer too. Sometimes God's answers to our prayers are *Yes!* and we quickly see him move. I love that! Other times, God says, *No, child. This isn't for you.* That can be tough, but it seems like the most frustrating answer is when God says, *Wait.*

Waiting can seem like such an inconvenience. A waste of time. A lost opportunity. We want to make things happen, feel productive, get things done! We can get impatient if something takes longer than, well, seconds. We soothe our can't-sit-still selves by constantly moving, so if we do have to wait, we don't feel like we are. We look at our watches, pull out our phones, and work to fill every slow moment with what seems like progress. This pseudo busyness gives us a false sense of achievement.

Now, let me say this: "waiting" should never be used as an excuse for not moving—for procrastinating or

dillydallying—when the light is green and God is saying
Go! You have nothing to wait for when you know he's calling you to move, even if you're afraid to step on the gas.

No, the kind of waiting I'm getting at is when there is
nothing for you to do but sit and wait, when no answer,
solution, email, phone call, or decision will change the
light to green. Unless you choose to take a side street
you know is not God's will, you have no choice but to be
still.

Susan's husband had an affair five years ago and left her
with three young children. Refusing to file for divorce,
she chose to wait, pray, and believe God for him to
come home. She's still waiting.

My friend Ashley was diagnosed with a life-threatening
disease this past year and is now dealing with the chal-
lenges of chemotherapy. She has amazing faith and trust
in God, and she's always smiling when I see her, yet she
would love to be well and strong. She keeps waiting.

Kate and Marc want to adopt another baby. Their profile
has now been passed over by two expectant mothers.
They aren't sure when their dream of adopting another
baby will come true. They just keep waiting.

Okay, it's your turn. What are *you* waiting for?

I am waiting for _____.

The word *wait* means to rest, to stay in one place, to be still. Why is that so hard? It sort of sounds like a vacation to me! So why is it so difficult to do? The reason is simple. We like to be in control. We like to set the clock for when things should happen—to decide for ourselves when the light turns green. The problem is not in the waiting; the problem is whether we really trust God in the times of waiting. We worry and wonder, *Has he forgotten me? Has he moved on and left me here . . . forever?*

I know it's hard to imagine, but if you're walking with God, seeking to do his will, and yet he's asking you to wait, this waiting season has a purpose. Even though your situation seems motionless, God isn't! He works behind the scenes, moving people and things into position for your good and your future. He wants to use this slow season to teach you, protect you, bless you, and strengthen your faith and trust in him.

Here are three things we learn in prayer when we wait:

1. *We learn to be persistent.* Paul wrote to the church in Colossae, "Since the day we heard about you, *we have not stopped* praying for you. We

continually ask God to fill you with the knowledge of his will" (Colossians 1:9 NIV, emphasis mine). Like anything else, patient and persistent prayer takes practice and determination. What better time to learn this than in times of waiting?

2. *We learn to trust God.* We know God sees the big picture while we only see what's right in front of us. In times of waiting, we can trust that he is getting things ready, putting them in an order only he can see to give us what we ask for at the right time.

3. *We learn to follow God's way.* It's a human reaction to rush off and do something fast to resolve a situation. It's also human to want to do things our own way, in our own time. This habit causes us to think we're the masters of our own lives, that we can control everything around us. But this is an illusion. And sometimes God uses seasons of waiting to remind us who is really in control, who really knows best, and to align our lives with his ways.

Dear girl, if you are struggling right now with a season of waiting, part of the difficulty might be that you're finding it a challenge to believe God is planning something good on the other side. Are you afraid your patient waiting is for nothing? The truth is that even when it doesn't feel like your hopes and dreams are moving forward, God is still working in response to your prayers. He isn't just preparing to bless you in the future; he wants to bless you right now, in the middle of your waiting! He has important things for you to know, learn, and experience in the waiting.

I love the promise in Isaiah 30:18, and I believe it's for you: "Blessed (happy, fortunate, to be envied) are *all* those who [earnestly] wait for Him, who expect and look and long for Him" (AMPC, emphasis mine).

Read those words again. Do you see what they're saying? That annoying stoplight is actually part of God's blessing. He is ahead of you, working out details and putting the pieces together. And he's with you now, teaching and enriching your prayer life in this season of waiting. So let me encourage you to stop looking frantically for a side street and revving your engine in frustration. Just take a deep breath, sit back in your seat, and press into this season of patient prayer. Because I can promise you this: *even when you're not moving, God still is.*

Are you waiting for something? Consider what God might be showing or teaching you in this time of waiting. As you pray today, ask him to help you see what he wants to reveal to you and to give you the grace and strength to wait with hope and expectation.

Copy this verse and put it in a place where you'll see it every day: "Let all that I am wait quietly before God, for my hope is in him" (Psalm 62:5).

Stars in the Night

I will give you treasures hidden in the darkness—
    secret riches.
I will do this so you may know that I am the LORD
    . . . the one who calls you by name.

ISAIAH 45:3

There is something magnificent about a clear midnight sky. Hidden behind the light of day are treasures to behold—treasures we would never, ever see without the darkness. I think God put them there, those twinkling jewels called stars, to remind us that whenever the lights in our lives grow dim, we need not fear. He is still there, ready to reveal treasures in the darkness of the night.

You most likely heard the words "Be home before dark!" as a child. Whether intended or not, some things we were taught as we walked through childhood subtly instilled in us a fear of the dark. And some of that is a good and healthy fear that keeps us safe and from running into things or falling. Light is necessary and good. Light reveals the beauty of color. Light shows us what's happening all around us. Light helps us find the contact lens we dropped on the floor. Sunlight keeps us warm and makes the trees, flowers, and plants grow. Light is important to everyday living! But God didn't just make the light; he made the darkness too. He even gave it a name. Genesis 1 says, "God spoke: 'Light!' And light appeared. God saw that light was good and separated light from dark. God named the light Day, and he named the dark Night" (verse 3 MSG).

Those words are *so* incredible to me! The Bible says that before God created light and made the day, the earth was formless and "darkness covered the deep waters" (verse 2). The universe was without any light, and God was just hanging out in his glory. And then—*drum roll, please*—out from the dark emptiness, by his creative power and might, God changed everything when he said these words: "Let there be light" (verse 3). In an instant, light split the blackness.

Have you ever wondered why God didn't choose to do away with darkness altogether? Why did he choose to create the night sky? He could very well have shouted out into the emptiness, "Let there be light—and no more darkness," eliminating darkness completely and permanently. But he didn't.

A few years ago, my daughter, Savannah, came walking into the kitchen to find me. "Mom! Have you been outside tonight?" Her tone was dramatic and insistent. "You need to see this!" We walked together onto the patio and into the night. "Look up!" she said, grinning. At first, I couldn't see much of anything; a glowing haze from the lights I'd left behind obscured my vision. But then as my eyes adjusted to the clear, moonless night, something amazing happened. There in the darkness, a thousand treasures came dancing into view. It was glorious.

"Aren't the stars incredible?" Savannah whispered.

For a few minutes, the two of us just stood there in wonder, looking at the sky. Like diamonds displayed on a gigantic black velvet canvas, the twinkling stars revealed their brilliance right before our eyes. I will never forget how beautiful it was.

When we walk through trials in life, we can feel as though we're wandering lost in the dark. But that night I was reminded that the God who made the light made the darkness too. The darkness was designed; it had a purpose—to reveal things like hidden treasures to us.

Isaiah 45:3 says, "I will give you treasures hidden in the darkness—secret riches. I will do this so you may know that I am the LORD, the God of Israel, the one who calls you by name." Verse 7 says, "I create the light and make the darkness."

That evening when Savannah and I stargazed, I was two months into a long and difficult recovery from breast cancer and a double mastectomy. I had been told that I would be up and feeling normal within two weeks of the surgery, but that wasn't the case. Savannah had to convince me to go outside that night, and as we walked, she had to hold my arm to steady me. There I was, nearly eight weeks post-surgery, dealing with seemingly endless complications, discomfort, and physical weakness. The truth is I didn't care one bit about having my boobs anymore. All I wanted was to get back to my life. I missed feeling strong. I was in the middle of walking through my own personal night of darkness.

In the middle of the night, when I didn't even have the strength to pray, God's reassuring presence became a treasure to my soul. More than ever, I knew I needed to hold on to his hand, to focus my heart on the truth of his Word. So that's what I did. As I lay in bed, I would rest my phone next to my pillow, listening to worship music and psalms being read to me. I couldn't do anything on my own to change the situation I was in. I had nothing and no one else to look to but God.

And there, in the stillness of my dark circumstance, he reminded me that his presence alone is all I need for every situation. That he is my life, my breath, my hope, my everything.

God has precious and personal things he wants to reveal to you when you walk through difficult and dark times— things about his character that you might not have noticed, like his comfort and protection for your heart. There in the dark you are more in tune with his voice. There your faith and trust in him grow stronger. There you are reminded of the importance of having people in your life to surround you with prayer, support, and encouragement—we need each other. And there you learn to have empathy for those around you who also walk through trials. Darkness reminds you what is ultimately most important: your relationship with God and family and having a faith-filled sisterhood around you.

> God has precious and personal things he wants to reveal to you when you walk through difficult and dark times.

Whatever you're experiencing or walking through, you're not alone. I encourage you to rest in the presence of the one who created both light and darkness. Even when you can't see your way, he's right there. And just like the stars in the night sky, rich and glorious treasures are there to be discovered when you look up to him in the dark.

Again, Isaiah 45:3 says, "I will give you treasures hidden in the darkness—secret riches. I will do this so you may know that I am the LORD . . . the one who calls you by name."[1]

What treasures did God reveal to your heart when you walked through a dark and challenging time? How did they strengthen your faith and your prayer life? What aspect of God's character became more real to you? Why?

SHE PRAYS
Power

WITH

PART FOUR

High Powered

I also pray that you will understand the incredible greatness of God's power for us who believe in him.

EPHESIANS 1:19

God's power. Do you ever stop to think about it? Thinking about his power builds our faith and reminds us not only of his awesome greatness but how his power is within us and works through our believing prayers.

Romans 1:20 says, "Ever since the world was created, people have seen the earth and sky. Through everything God made, they can clearly see his invisible qualities—his *eternal power* and divine nature" (emphasis mine). God puts his power and might on display so we will believe him and know that his power is available to us every day.

God's power was there at the creation of the world. Everything we see around us came to be by his mighty power, and his power is what holds everything together. That's a big deal! With just a word, God created the universe. Right now, in this second, his mighty hands are holding a billion stars and a million galaxies in place. And by his power he is lighting and warming the earth with the sun.

Let's just stop for a second and think about the sun, such an incredible part of his creation. Every single day, it sends 240 trillion horsepower of energy to light and warm and power the earth. That's over 30,000 horsepower of energy for each person on the planet. God's provision of free energy power is abundant beyond belief!

Then there's the earth. With the tip of his finger, he spins it at about 67,000 miles per hour as it orbits around the sun.[1] What a wild ride we're on—*amazing!* And on top of all that, God's power gives breath and life to every human being—including you.

All that power—the same power that was there at the beginning of time, that sets the world in motion and holds everything in place—is available to you every day. God not only wants you to understand that his power is yours; he also wants you fully connected to his power for every part of your life.

Listen to what Paul wrote to the church in Ephesus: "I also pray that you will understand the incredible greatness of God's power for us who believe him. This is the same mighty power that raised Christ from the dead and seated him in the place of honor at God's right hand in the heavenly realms" (Ephesians 1:19–20). This was Paul's prayer for all believers. He knew it was essential for us to comprehend that the moment we put our faith in Jesus, God's power becomes vibrant and active in our lives. This idea of God's power in us, working through us, isn't some fairy-tale, make-you-feel-good, self-help crutch to make it through the day. No! This is real, supernatural, plugged-into-the-creator-of-the-universe kind of power.

My friend, because you're a believer, God's power lives in you! His will is for you to consciously and constantly connect to his power so that his glory and supernatural work will show in your life and in your prayers. His power should be as real to you as the sun's light and warmth that surround your day.

One of the saddest things I see in ministry is girls living weak and powerless lives as believers. Instead of living victoriously, visibly empowered by the Holy Spirit (Acts 1:8; Romans 8:9) who lives within them, they limp along, unaware that as a daughter of their heavenly Father, they have access to his strength and supernatural power! It breaks my heart to watch girls walking around struggling day after day to be strong when they were made to be prayer warriors, leaders, and confident women of God!

You, my dear girl, were designed to live empowered, strong, confident, and mighty in Christ Jesus! But you have to be fully connected to receive and experience his power.

Jesus told his followers that if they wanted to experience God's fullness, they had to be fully connected. He said, "Live in me. Make your home in me just as I do in you. . . . I am the Vine, you are the branches. When you're joined with me [plugged into his power] and I with you . . . the harvest is sure to be abundant. Separated, you can't produce a thing" (John 15:4–5 MSG). The English Standard Version of the Bible puts it this way in verse 7: "If you abide in me." If you abide in Christ, then you will see God's power at work in your life. The word *abide* means to be fully connected. To further reveal the importance of our need to be fully connected, Jesus uses the illustration of a branch being connected to the vine. If a branch isn't attached to the vine, it receives no sustenance, no strength, no power to flourish or survive. And disconnected, it will eventually die.

If you're feeling powerless, it's not because God is weakened. His power never fades, and he never changes. He's always faithful, no matter what. If you're struggling to be strong, you need to check your connection by

She Prays with Power

spending time in the Word and by abiding in his presence through prayer. It's like when a lamp's cord loosens from a power outlet, interrupting the electrical current that powers the lamp. The darkness isn't the power's fault; the power is still there. But a weak connection resulted in the loss of power and light. Ephesians 6:10 says, "Be strong in the Lord and in his mighty power." We can choose to "be strong," to walk in the power and strength God provides.

As a believer in Jesus, you're plugged in to the source of divine power. And as you go to God in prayer, that power is activated in your life. Yet you choose how connected you want to be. What I want you to realize is that God's supernatural power is in you, and through prayer his power is activated in a way that affects your life and the lives of everyone around you.

If you need strength today, pray. If you need healing today, pray. If you need protection today, pray. If you need to be set free from bondage today, pray. If you need help with your parenting, pray. If you need restoration of your marriage, pray. If you need a miracle, pray. Prayer will connect you to God's power and to your miracle!

Prayer will connect you to God's power and to your miracle!

Let me leave you with this from 2 Peter 1:3: "By his divine *power*, God has given us

182

everything we need for living a godly life. We have received all of this by coming to know him" (emphasis mine).

Whatever you're struggling against, battling, facing, or needing is no match for God's power. Always remember that you have a direct connection with the greatest power source in the universe, and by that power you can live a victorious life in his glorious name.

———

During your prayer time today, read Paul's words in Ephesians 1:19–20. What do you see in those verses that gives you confidence to walk in victory and believe for a miracle no matter what you're facing today? God's Word gives us specific examples of what his power can do in your life:

- Strengthen you in weakness. (Isaiah 40:29–31)
- Deliver you from evil. (James 4:7)
- Protect you from harm. (Psalm 118:5–9)
- Heal your body from sickness and pain. (James 5:13–15)
- Set you free from sin and bondage. (Galatians 5:1)

Be That Girl

**Awake, O my soul, with the music of his splendor.
Arise, my soul, and sing his praises!**

PSALM 108:1–2 TPT

Have you ever ended up somewhere you had no intention of being and thought, *This is not what I planned*? I have.

A few years ago, John, Savannah, and I were riding bikes on a trail along the Eagle River in Colorado. It was a gorgeous, sunny day in the mountains, and we were having a blast, zooming down the path on our motorized bikes. About twenty minutes into our exhilarating adventure, John noticed the perfect place for us to stop and take a picture—a rocky ledge overlooking the river.

As I went to dismount, my tennis shoe got stuck on the seat of the bike and simultaneously my other foot slid on the rocks. The next thing I knew I was on the ground, unable to move and in excruciating pain.

I was sure something was horribly wrong, and I was right. I had shattered my pelvis. The hospital would be my home for the next two weeks. Needless to say, this was not what I had planned.

In Acts 16, two men found themselves in a place they hadn't planned to be. Paul and Silas had made their way to the city of Philippi on a mission to spread the gospel when they were wrongly accused of causing an uprising. Within minutes, they went from being free men doing good for others to being beaten, tortured, and thrown into a dark and filthy prison cell. They were in severe pain and without any light, and they didn't know how or when they would be set free. This was definitely not on their agenda.

But Paul and Silas had made an important choice way before this unexpected moment. They had determined to trust God no matter what came their way. Acts 16:25 says that "around midnight, Paul and Silas were praying and singing." Their faith-filled prayers turned into songs of praise. I don't know about you, but I find that almost unbelievable. These guys were in a pitch-black, stinky cell with who knows what scurrying around their feet.

Their backs were bloody, and they quite possibly had broken bones from being beaten. Yet they were singing praises to God! I can't help but wonder who started singing first, and I can only imagine what the other prisoners and the guards were thinking as they listened to these two men.

Paul was a prayer and praise warrior. His message in 1 Thessalonians 5:16–18 reveals his commitment to living with an attitude of thankfulness and praise to God no matter what he faced: rejoice always, pray continually, give thanks in all circumstances. This was his motto, this is how he lived, and this is what he knew would give him victory through any trial.

We don't know the exact words Paul and Silas prayed that night. They might have prayed for God to set them free. They might have prayed for the pain to end. They might have prayed for the prisoners around them to be saved. We don't know. But we do know their prayers were full of faith and gratitude, and as they lifted their voices to God, their words turned to a melody of worship that resounded throughout that prison. Heaven took notice.

Prayers mixed with praise change everything. Listen to what happened next in the story: "Suddenly, there was a massive earthquake, and the prison was shaken to its foundation. All the doors immediately flew open, and the chains of every prisoner fell off! The jailer woke up to see the prison doors wide open" (Acts 16:26–27).

In verses 29–30, the Bible goes on to say that "the jailer called for the lights and ran to the dungeon and fell down trembling before Paul and Silas. Then he brought them out and asked, 'Sirs, what must I do to be saved?'"

Because of their praise, Paul and Silas saw miracles happen. Their praise brought God's supernatural power into their situation. Not only were they set free but the lives of people around them were transformed by their faith-filled worship.

I want to ask you two questions: Do you make a practice of praising God every day? And as with Paul and Silas, are your prayers mixed with praise when you find yourself in a difficult situation?

After my accident, I was airlifted home from Colorado and admitted to a rehab hospital. I would love to say it was easy to keep an attitude of praise, but it wasn't. Yet I made the choice to rejoice. Many days were hard and painful. One night in particular, nearly three weeks into my recovery, I was horribly sick from medication withdrawal. I was so sick that I couldn't move. John and Savannah had been sitting by my bedside for hours, praying and trying everything they could to help me.

Sometime late in the night, Savannah began to sing praises to God, filling the room with worship. And then a miracle happened. God's presence flooded my exhausted body and mind with his peace, my pain and discomfort eased, and I fell fast asleep. The praise that came from Savannah's heart that night was from a well of worship that lives deep inside her. This was not something she manufactured for that moment. This is how she lives.

I love worshipping and praising God. I love what it does for my soul. Praise isn't always easy, but it is powerful. And making praise and worship a part of your prayer life not only will change how you pray; it will also change you. When you make praise a habit, your life takes on a whole new dimension of joy and thanksgiving. You start the day believing in good things. You praise God for your children as you get them ready for school. You praise him for your clothes as you fold them. You praise him for your job as you drive to work. You praise him for your car that needs new tires. You praise him because he is worthy, because he is good, and because of his love for you.

You can praise God for so much—an endless list. And if you make it a habit to praise him when you pray, your prayers will rise to a new level of faith. Like Paul and Silas, you will pray believing God is going to help you! And even when life is difficult, you will find your prayers turning to praise in your car, in your home, at work, at school, in your church, and even in the hospital will change everything.

If you need a miracle, try praising God in faith even before you can see how the chains of your circumstances are going to be unlocked.

Praise isn't always easy, but it is powerful.

If your day is going poorly, praise God. If you need a breakthrough in your marriage, praise God. If you're being persecuted in your workplace, praise God. If you need a financial miracle, praise God.

As I write these words, I feel convicted to praise God more, to be a girl who's known for having joy in every situation and praising God no matter what happens! I want to be the girl who has stories to tell of how heaven came down in the middle of her prayers of praise and changed everything! How about you?

The book of Psalms is filled with words of praise to God. Read Psalm 34:1–10 and use it as a template to create a poem or a letter or even to draw something representing your gratitude and thankfulness to God. As you do, enjoy his presence and watch how praise connects your heart to his in a unique and powerful way.

If today you feel as though you are in a prison of circumstances and find it difficult to form words of praise, I want you to know that I've been there. Don't be too hard on yourself. God understands your hurting heart. I encourage you to turn on worship music and just sit and listen to the words. Play it all day long if you need to. Let it fill your heart and mind. You'll be amazed at how God's presence will saturate your home and begin to open your heart again to praise him.

Knock, Knock

Yet because of his impudence he will rise and give him whatever he needs.

LUKE 11:8 ESV

Look at today's verse. Do you notice the word *impudence*? Now, that's not a word you see every day. And interestingly enough, this is the only time it's used in the New Testament. To be impudent is to be brazen, audacious, cheeky, nervy, bold, shameless—to have chutzpah.[1] What a feisty little word! It might not be a word you would think is associated with approaching God in prayer, but it is.

Jesus tells two different parables about this prayer attitude of shameless and bold persistence. The first one is in Luke 11. A man has surprise visitors come to the door of his house late one night, but his own pantry is empty, so he knocks on his neighbor's door to ask for bread to serve his guests. (Hospitality was a *big deal* in Middle Eastern culture.) His neighbor is so irritated that he doesn't even open the door but blurts out in exasperation, "Do you know what time it is? My family is already asleep. Go away."

Then Jesus said, "I tell you this—though he won't do it for friendship's sake, if you keep knocking long enough, he will get up and give you whatever you need because of your shameless persistence" (Luke 11:8).

Jesus used this parable to illustrate how we should approach our heavenly Father in prayer and how he will respond to us when we're shamelessly persistent in our praying. The people in the parable weren't even friends, and yet the neighbor would eventually give in to the persistent knocking and provide the man what he needed! This is how Jesus is encouraging us to pray— with shameless persistence and confident expectation.

How much more should we not give up in prayer knowing that God, our heavenly Father, is on the other side of our persistent knocking?

This same example of persistence is in Jesus's second parable in Luke 18. A widow went to a ruthless and unjust judge for help and said to him, "Give me justice in this dispute with my enemy" (verse 3). We're not told exactly what kind of situation she was in, but it's obvious that she was desperate and had no one to advocate for her. Although she pleaded with the judge, he refused to help her. However, she didn't give up. Over and over she begged him to take on her case. Finally, he said to himself, "I'm going to see that she gets justice, because she is wearing me out with her constant requests!" (verse 5).

This woman had moxie. You go, girl! It was her impudence and her audacity to keep on asking that finally convinced the judge to give her justice. I love this story! Her shamelessly persistent pleading, even when the odds were stacked against her, got her what she needed! Then Jesus brings the point home: "So don't you think God will surely give justice to his chosen people who cry out to him day and night? Will he keep putting them off? I tell you, he will grant justice to them quickly!" (verses 7–8).

Both of these parables teach us to persist in prayer—to never give up on going to God for our needs and to believe that he cares! Neither the man nor the widow gave up easily. And you know what? God is excited when he sees that kind of faith in us. He responds to our shameless persistence.

In the same way that little children completely trust their parents to take care of their every need, we can trust that God will always do what is best for us as his children. In Luke 11:11–13, Jesus said, "You fathers—if your children ask for a fish, do you give them a snake instead? Or if they ask for an egg, do you give them a scorpion? Of course not! So if you sinful people know how to give good gifts to your children, how much more will your heavenly Father give the Holy Spirit to those who ask him."

God is intrinsically good. Unlike humans, he doesn't do good things because he wants to look good or to impress people. He *is* good, and everything he does is good. The writer of Psalm 119:68 says to the Lord, "You are good and do only good." So when we remember this powerful and comforting fact about who he is, we can have perfect confidence that God is committed to do what's best for us. Like a little child, we can pray with all the boldness and all the audacity we can muster, knowing he will come through because God will always honor who he says he is.

> God is intrinsically good. Unlike humans, he doesn't do good things because he wants to look good or to impress people. He *is* good, and everything he does is good.

In 1998, as a church, we found ourselves in an exciting season. We had experienced tremendous growth and moved from one worship service to three. We were using every square inch of our building and parking lot. We had no choice—we had to build another building. But the land we felt God was directing us to build on was not for sale. That was definitely a problem.

This ideal piece of property was right off the highway (a prime spot) and just a few minutes from our current church building. However, the owners adamantly did not want to sell the land. It had been in their family since the Civil War, and they were committed to keeping it that way. But we didn't feel we should take no for an answer; we believed in our hearts that this was the land God wanted for us.

So John called the church to a three-day fast—to approach God with a bold, audacious faith just like the widow approached the judge, to keep knocking like the man! Three days after the fast, the family called us and said, "We changed our mind. Although the land is still not for sale, we will sell it to you. But only to you!" Wow. God honored our audacious faith and persistent knocking. He responded to our commitment to not give up! And God is no respecter of persons. Just like he honored our shamelessly persistent prayers, he will honor yours.

My friend, don't give up on those prayers you've been praying. Keep praying and keep believing, because God is going to honor your faith. Your answer might be just around the corner. Jesus ends the parable about the impudent neighbor with these words: "Keep on asking, and you will receive what you ask for. Keep on seeking, and you will find. Keep on knocking, and the door will be opened to you. For everyone who asks, receives. Everyone who seeks, finds. And to everyone who knocks, the door will be opened" (Luke 11:9–10).

Don't give up. Don't just go to God once and then quit praying. Do it over and over and over again until you get an answer. Mark Batterson, author of *The Circle Maker*, says it this way: "It's not our job to answer; it's our job to ask."[2]

Keep on asking and keep on asking and don't hold back!

Have you stopped praying about a need in your life because you didn't get an answer fast enough? Did you give up? Start knocking again. Ask God to build your faith today. Ask him to help you to not grow weary but to continue to seek him and trust him for an answer in his perfect time.

Always Expecting

DAY 29

Since we have this confidence, we can also have great boldness before him, for if we present any request agreeable to his will, he will hear us.

1 JOHN 5:14 TPT

One story in the Old Testament is about a man who had an incredible and beyond-ordinary faith—a faith that was not only persistent but overflowing with anticipation. His name was Elijah.

When we pick up this story in 1 Kings 18, we see that the land of Israel was experiencing a devastating drought. This isn't merely a dry spell; it had not rained for over three years. Elijah was a prophet at that time. In the middle of this long drought, God spoke to him and

197

said, "Go and present yourself to King Ahab. Tell him that I will soon send rain!" (verse 1).

Interestingly, following God's promise of rain, the famine grew more severe. But that didn't stop Elijah from believing what had been spoken to him. He expected God to be true to his word, but he didn't just sit on his faith. He began to speak as though the answer was coming, and he prayed. The Bible says Elijah told King Ahab, "Go get something to eat and drink, for I hear a mighty rainstorm coming!" (verse 41). So Ahab left, but Elijah got on his knees. There in the middle of impossible odds, with his knees in dry dirt and another cloudless sky over his head, Elijah knelt and prayed.

Have you ever been in a place like that? Where nothing was encouraging you to believe? Nothing. That was where Elijah was, yet without any visible sign of things changing, he began to voice his expectation for things to change—and he prayed and prayed and prayed. And as he prayed with expectation, he began to see rain, still without a cloud in the sky.

The Bible says he told his servant six times to go see if the rain was coming, but each time the servant came back and said he hadn't seen anything. Then the seventh time the servant came back with a wee bit of news: "Elijah, I saw a little cloud rising from the sea."

I can just hear the excitement in Elijah's voice in response to his servant's report: "That's awesome! I knew it would come! How big is it?"

And then the servant's sheepish response: "Well . . . [imagine a long hesitation], it's only about the size of a man's hand, sir."

The size of a hand! Think about that. It was an itty-bitty, teeny-weeny cloud.

Yet what does Elijah do? He puts on his raincoat and boots and tells his servant to hurry and go tell the king. He also tells him not to waste any time or he'd be caught in the rainstorm. The Bible says, "And soon the sky was black with clouds. A heavy wind brought a terrific rainstorm" (verse 45).

Elijah had faith crazy enough to believe that the little cloud was the miracle he'd been praying for—and it was.

John MacArthur wrote, "Faith hears the inaudible, sees the invisible, and does the impossible."[1] How does faith do that? What is the secret to having that kind of energized faith? Faith like Elijah's that sees and hears the answer before the answer comes? A faith that says, *I know God is working, even when I can't yet see how.* A faith that doesn't just pray but prays expecting something to happen.

We've talked about being persistent in prayer and how we need to be girls who have moxie when it comes to approaching God. Persistence and expectation are equally important for faith-filled praying. If you're praying all the time but don't truly expect God to do anything, you, my dear, are working hard but not seeing many results.

Hebrews 11:1 puts it this way: "Faith is the assurance of things hoped for, the conviction of things not seen" (ESV). Faith is being altogether sure that God will do what he says and convinced that he's working despite what you see. This faith, this unrelenting confidence, comes from a deep and conscious realization of who God is. We find that in one place: time in his presence, where God deposits a faith-filled expectancy in our hearts. And that knowledge of God inspires a hope that sees beyond the natural, beyond what is visible, to believe that he can do a miracle no matter what our physical eyes see around us. Expectant faith makes it possible to believe what is impossible to see.

I want to talk to you about faith for a minute. The fact that you're reading these words tells me you've got faith. More faith than you realize. If you aren't seeing God work in your life, the problem is not that you don't have faith; it's that you aren't using the faith you have to its fullest potential. The Bible says each of us has been given a measure of faith (Romans 12:3), and that it takes only a teeny tiny seed of faith (Matthew 17:20) to see God do amazing things in our lives. Yet it's our job to put our faith in action and purpose to live a life of expectation. We need to start praying confident prayers—proof that we really do believe God is listening and that he is going to respond.

James 5:17 says Elijah was a human "just like all of us." Those words, "just like all of us," are so encouraging to me. Why? Because when Elijah prayed, God noticed and responded in super-

> **It takes only a teeny tiny seed of faith to see God do amazing things in our lives.**

natural ways, and yet Elijah wasn't any different from you and me. This guy wasn't some kind of superhero; he was a normal person who believed God more than most.

Seventeen years ago, God called me to start a women's conference. He gave me a vision of thousands of women gathering in one place. I thought, *How could that ever be possible?* I didn't have the ability, talent, or resources, and I wasn't at all confident to lead. I didn't know where to begin. Yet I knew what he had whispered to my heart one day in prayer: *Debbie, if you will believe and trust me, someday thousands of women are going to gather, and you will be leading them.*

So I started praying, asking him to show me what to do and to give me the faith for what he was speaking to my heart. One year later, a group of faith-filled girls came alongside me, and we launched the Designed for Life Women's Conference with 378 girls! God breathed on it, and we have seen it grow continually. Now, sixteen years later, more than ten thousand women gather every year! Yet I believe there is still more, and I'm expecting that God will do it.

One of my favorite verses in the Bible is Ephesians 3:20: "God can do anything, you know—far more than you could ever imagine or guess or request in your wildest dreams!" (MSG).

God loves the thrill of surprising us when we believe him. He loves showing off his glory and his power. He loves to come down and reveal himself to girls who are expecting out-of-this-world answers—answers that anticipate him doing something beyond the natural, beyond what they can do themselves. Something impossible.

Have you been given an impossible dream or an out-of-this-world hope? If God has placed something in your heart, then perhaps it's time to take it seriously and start praying about it. Following Elijah's example of persistent, expectant prayer, set a reminder on your phone to pray every day for the next seven days about this God dream or miracle you're believing for. Then watch the sky for rain!

Always Expecting

Now Act Like It

The Kingdom of God is not just a lot of talk; it is living by God's power.

1 CORINTHIANS 4:20

We know that when we pray, we connect to the awesome power of God, the power of his word that set creation into motion and holds the entire universe in place. Prayer activates the same power that's proclaimed and revealed in story after story in the Bible—calming storms, halting the sun in its path, routing armies, healing the blind, raising the dead, and on and on. But you know that power was never meant to stay in our prayers. It's designed to go through us to do God's good work.

A vibrant prayer life is intended to motivate you to an active, aggressive, intentional way of living. Your time in God's presence will strengthen your faith and lead you to action. A faith lived out in your everyday life is evidence of the work of God's power in you. James 2:14–17 asks, "What good is it, dear brothers and sisters, if you say you have faith but don't show it by your actions? Can that kind of faith save anyone? Suppose you see a brother or sister who has no food or clothing, and you say, 'Good-bye and have a good day; stay warm and eat well'—but then you don't give that person any food or clothing. What good does that do? So you see, faith by itself isn't enough. Unless it produces good deeds, it is dead and useless."

A prayer life that is alive, growing, and powered by faith is designed to be seen and heard. Your faith should be visible to others not just at church, but at school, work, home, the grocery store, and the gym. It shouldn't be a surprise to those around you that you are a believer. Rather, your love and commitment to God should be evident to those you live with, work with, and spend time with.

> **A prayer life that is alive, growing, and powered by faith is designed to be seen and heard.**

There is a short story in the book of Acts about when two of Jesus's disciples, Peter and John, were arrested and taken to court for preaching the gospel. The two men spoke with boldness, and as their accusers listened, "they recognized that [Peter and John] had been with Jesus" even though "they were ordinary men with no special training in the Scriptures" (Acts 4:13 ESV). How beautiful that the faith of these two men, obvious in their actions and words, was so strong that it marked them as friends of Jesus.

In John 14:12–14, Jesus said, "I tell you the truth, anyone who believes in me will do the same works I have done, and even greater works, because I am going to be with the Father. You can ask for anything in my name, and I will do it, so that the Son can bring glory to the Father. Yes, ask me for anything in my name, and I will do it!" Jesus is clearly talking to the disciples as if the "doing" is a given—*of course* they're going to go and do. I mean, the disciples spending all that time hearing Jesus's teaching and then never actually doing anything would be totally crazy!

See, Jesus wasn't interested in raising up spiritual couch potatoes. He taught the disciples to pray, but he also commanded them to go. Their prayers and time with God were meant to fuel them to go out into the world, share the good news of Jesus, and minister to others. Jesus called them to put action behind their beliefs, to encourage the brothers and sisters in the faith, and to touch the lives of those around them with the same love and grace they received from God, so that, in turn, others would come to faith in him.

You have the same power in you that Jesus did, my dear. Yes, you read that right. By your prayers and faith, it's possible for you to see the same signs and wonders the disciples witnessed. As you grow closer to God, you will learn to respond to a lost and hurting world with the power he's given you.

My friend is such a good example of this. She's a reporter for a news station in our city. Every day she's surrounded by opposition, ridiculed and scorned for her commitment to follow Jesus. But that doesn't deter her from sharing the gospel. I asked her how she has the strength to share Jesus in such difficult and often hostile situations. She told me, "Every day, I must begin with prayer. This is what I pray:

> "Lord, may I always remember that the fight is against the enemy of our souls, not against the people around me. You love them and you are for them! Your heart is to reconcile all people to you, even the ones who seem hostile. You call the most distant souls home to you. Help me to believe despite what I see! Increase my faith to confidently trust that it is your will for them to be saved. Help me to believe that I will see you work through me. Lord, as I enter the war zone today, equip me for the battle. May only your words be on my lips, and may your Spirit in me point others to Jesus. Amen."

Through her prayers, God is obviously giving her strength. She is one of the most faith-filled and actively passionate-about-God girls I have ever known. She never backs down from her commitment to be a witness, no matter what.

God's power and love were always meant to be shared through our words and actions. But remember, we don't live out our faith on our own energy. It is God who works in us and through us. It's *his* power. He will help us know what to do and how to make the most of the opportunities he gives us. Ephesians 5:15–17 encourages you and me with these words: "Be careful how you live. Don't live like fools, but like those who are wise. Make the most of every opportunity in these evil days. Don't act thoughtlessly, but understand what the Lord wants you to do."

My friend, just think about how far you've come since beginning this journey! But it doesn't stop here. Your faith is on the rise. It's been growing for a while, and now it's time to put it into action. Here's my challenge to you: don't keep what God is doing in your life to yourself! Take hold of this beautiful gift of witnessing God's power working in you and seize the amazing opportunity to be his hands and feet to a world in need.

Read Isaiah 61:1–2:

> The Spirit of the Sovereign Lord is upon me,
>   for the Lord has anointed me

> to bring good news to the poor.
> He has sent me to comfort the brokenhearted
>   and to proclaim that captives will be released
>   and prisoners will be freed.
> He has sent me to tell those who mourn
>   that the time of the LORD's favor has come,
>   and with it, the day of God's anger against their
>   enemies.

These verses present a powerful picture of what happens when God, through his Holy Spirit, works through us. Underline the actions found in these verses that reveal the power of God in the world. How might you personally put these actions into practice in your own community and circle of influence?

"Bring good news to the poor" =

_____

"Comfort the brokenhearted" =

_____

"Proclaim that captives will be released" =

_____

The Blessing

Blessed is she who has believed that the Lord would fulfill his promises to her!

LUKE 1:45 NIV

For the past eight years, my husband, John, has closed every Sunday morning service the same way. After we have worshipped and prayed together, listened to the message, and heard the invitation for salvation, the auditorium goes silent with expectation. He extends his hands, and with his strong and confident voice, he prays this prayer of blessing from Numbers 6:24–26 over the people:

> May the LORD bless you
> and protect you.

> May the LORD smile on you
> > and be gracious to you.
> May the LORD show you his favor
> > and give you his peace.

God loves to bless people. He loves to go before them, to help them, to care for them, to provide for everything they need. And he loves for them to expect and anticipate his goodness to be poured out on their lives.

And God wants to bless you, my friend.

He has revealed so many things over these thirty-one days. He has taken you into a deeper understanding of prayer and given you more boldness and confidence to believe your prayers have power to change your life and the world around you. Yet if I want you to always remember one thing, it's that God loves to set his hand of blessing on your life!

The Bible reminds us over and over that as we honor him with our whole heart, commit to listening for his voice, and submit to his will, God's blessing and favor will be a part of our lives:

- Blessed (highly favored) is the one who delights in the Lord. (Psalm 37:4)
- Blessed and greatly favored is the one who finds his strength in God. (Psalm 84:5)
- God wants to bless his people abundantly—in all things. (2 Corinthians 9:8)

- God supplies our needs through his treasure of unending riches. (Philippians 4:19)
- Our heavenly Father loves to give us good and perfect gifts. (James 1:17)

Scripture is full of stories about people who experienced God's blessing on their lives.

Abraham followed God, and God blessed his faithful obedience, saying, "I will make you into a great nation. I will bless you and make you famous, and you will be a blessing to others" (Genesis 12:2).

Joseph, despite being sold into slavery by his brothers, chose to forgive them and honor God with his life. And God blessed him and elevated his influence in ways he never dreamed possible.

Ruth followed God's leading to go with her mother-in-law, Naomi, to a different country, to a new life. God honored her loyalty and her commitment to him. He led her to Boaz, a godly man who loved and provided for her, and God blessed them with a baby boy who would be the grandfather of King David.

And then there's one of my favorite Bible characters of all—Mary, the mother of Jesus. You probably know her story. Her life is such a powerful and beautiful example of how God will bless a girl who completely surrenders to his will. Mary was just like you and me, with dreams about what her life would be like. When the angel showed up to speak with her, Mary was engaged to be married. She had probably imagined what her wedding day would be like and how she would look in her dress dancing with her new husband, Joseph.

Yet God, through the angel Gabriel, comes to her and says, "You have found favor with God! You will conceive and give birth to a son, and you will name him Jesus" (Luke 1:30–31). God calls Mary to something far different from what she had planned. It would take faith for her to follow his leading. She would be ridiculed and face hardship and difficulty for accepting God's plan for her. But she had a choice. Would she trust and follow God? Would she believe that no matter what he called her to do, he would be with her, go before her, and watch over her with love and care? And, yes, *bless* her?

One of the most powerful statements in all of Scripture is Mary's response to what she heard from God: "I am the Lord's servant. May everything you have said about me come true" (verse 38). Think about that response. She knew what she was giving up—her desires, her freedom to choose her path, and her own will. She was saying to God, "I want your will over mine, and I trust you completely." And then we see the Lord's response to her in Luke 1:45, spoken through her cousin Elizabeth: "Blessed [spiritually fortunate and favored by God] is she who believed and confidently trusted . . . the things that were spoken to her [by the angel sent] from the Lord" (AMP).

God's blessing over Mary wasn't given to her because of her knowledge or because of her upbringing, ability, or talent. It was based on her faith and trust in him. This ordinary girl from an ordinary place found favor with God because she desired to do his will more than anything else.

I want to ask you a question. Do you believe God wants to bless you? Listen to this: "The eyes of the Lord search the whole earth in order to strengthen those whose hearts are fully committed to him" (2 Chronicles 16:9). God's blessing is for everyone and anyone who commits to him with their whole heart. He isn't looking for a girl with a perfect past. He isn't looking for a girl who thinks she's talented. He isn't looking for a girl who feels like she has it all together. He isn't searching for a girl who never, ever fails or makes a mistake. He's looking for a girl just like you—one who believes his Word, who seeks after him with all her heart, and is fully committed to doing his will.

God doesn't want to bless only those people in the Bible. He doesn't want to keep his blessing for preachers or Bible teachers. He longs to bless every girl. He wants to bless *you*, and, in turn, to bless others through you. Your trust, your commitment—and just like Mary, your faith—will open the windows of heaven over your life to receive God's blessing.

Your prayers are like your own personal prophecies. News flash! In many ways, the words you pray over yourself, your family, and your circumstances determine the trajectory of your life. As your faith grows in God's Word and you spend time in his presence, through time your prayers will begin to transform—changing from small, anemic, all-about-me prayers to big, expectant, faith-filled prayers. And those prayers of blessing will tremendously affect everyone around you. Psalm 31:19 says, "How great is the goodness you have stored up for those who fear you. You lavish it on those who come to you for protection, *blessing them before the watching world*" (emphasis mine).

What a beautiful promise. Your life was meant to show-case God's goodness and his salvation to the world. God created you and designed your life to display his extraordinary love and power—and his blessing.

What if, at the close of this devotional journey, you made a commitment to believe God on a whole new level? What if you decided to trust in his plans for your life every day, saying, *Not my will, but yours, God!* And what if, from this day on, you prayed with a bold confidence, believing that God's power is at work in you to do more through you than ever before?

As you choose to live a fully committed, completely trusting, and confidently believing life, your prayers *will have power*. God's blessing and favor *will follow you*. And you *will see him* move in ways you never, ever imagined.

First Corinthians 2:9 says, "Things which the eye has not seen and the ear has not heard, and which have not entered the heart of man, all that God has prepared for those who love him [who hold Him in affectionate reverence, who obey Him, and who gratefully recognize the benefits that He has bestowed]" (AMP).

And that, my dear, is my prayer for you!

And now,

> May the LORD bless you
>   and protect you.
> May the LORD smile on you
>   and be gracious to you.
> May the LORD show you his favor
>   and give you his peace.
>
> Amen.

The Blessing

Notes

Foreword

1. John Calvin, quoted in Richard J. Foster, *Prayer* (San Francisco: Harper-Collins, 1992), 197.

Day 1 An Open Door

1. Simon Holley, *Sustainable Power* (Cambridge: Authentic Media, 2013), chap. 1, Kindle.

Day 2 It Starts Here

1. "Found by Jesus, and Finding Jesus," *The Complete Works of C. H. Spurgeon*, accessed April 29, 2019, https://www.spurgeongems.org /vols40-42/chs2375.pdf.

Day 5 A Daughter's Cry

1. Max Lucado, "God's Favorite Name is 'Father,'" MaxLucado.com, July 2016, https://maxlucado.com/gods-favorite-name-father/.

Day 12 What's His Name?

1. John Piper, "Hallowed Be Thy Name: In All the Earth," sermon, November 4, 1984, https://www.desiringgod.org/messages/hallowed-be -thy-name-in-all-the-earth.

2. Piper, "Hallowed Be Thy Name."

Day 16 Surprise Trash

1. Dietrich Bonhoeffer, *The Cost of Discipleship* (New York: Touchstone, 1995), 163.

Day 17 He Did So You Can

1. Andrew Murray, "Chapter 4—After This Manner Pray or the Model Prayer," Worthy Christian Library, accessed April 29, 2019, https://www .worthychristianlibrary.com/andrew-murray/with-christ-in-the-school-of -prayer/chapter-4-after-this-manner-pray-or-the-model-prayer/.

2. Corrie ten Boom, "Guideposts Classics: Corrie ten Boom on Forgiveness," *Guideposts*, July 24, 2014, https://www.guideposts.org/better-living /positive-living/guideposts-classics-corrie-ten-boom-on-forgiveness.

Day 19 Deliver Us

1. Leonard Ravenhill, "Leonard Ravenhill Quotes," AZ Quotes, accessed April 29, 2019, https://www.azquotes.com/quote/673496.

Day 20 This One Thing

1. Martin Luther, "Martin Luther Quotes," Goodreads, accessed April 29, 2019, https://www.goodreads.com/author/quotes/29874.Martin_Luther.

Day 21 I Hear You

1. Debbie Lindell, *She Believes* (Grand Rapids: Revell, 2016), 236.

2. Lindell, 237.

Day 22 1, 2, 3 . . . Rest

1. *Oxford Dictionaries*, s.v. "anxiety," accessed March 22, 2019, https://en .oxforddictionaries.com/definition/anxiety.

2. Anxiety and Depression Association of America, "Facts and Statistics," accessed March 22, 2019, http://adaa.org/about-adaa/press-room/facts -statistics.

Day 25 Stars in the Night

1. Portions taken from Lindell, *She Believes*, chap. 11.

Day 26 High Powered

1. Matt Rosenberg, "Speed of the Earth," ThoughtCo., February 13, 2018, https://www.thoughtco.com/speed-of-the-earth-1435093.

Day 28 Knock, Knock

1. See *Oxford English Dictionary*, s.v. "impudence," accessed April 26, 2019, https://en.oxforddictionaries.com/thesaurus/impudence.

2. Mark Batterson, *Draw the Circle: The 40-Day Prayer Challenge* (Grand Rapids: Zondervan, 2012), 45.

Day 29 Always Expecting

1. John MacArthur Jr., *Hebrews: The MacArthur New Testament Commentary* (Chicago: Moody, 1983), 332.

Debbie Lindell is the author of *She Believes*. She and her husband, John, serve as lead pastors of James River Church in Springfield, Missouri. In 2003, Debbie launched the Designed for Life Women's Conference, which today draws ten thousand women annually from across the nation and around the world. This flourishing sisterhood reflects the passion of her heart—encompassing women from all walks of life who celebrate one another through a life-giving and authentic connection. Find out more about Debbie and the Designed Sisterhood at DebbieLindell.com.

LET'S STAY CONNECTED!

What a joy it has been to share this prayer journey with you. I believe we were created for connection and that sisterhood is a gift from heaven! It represents the beauty of relationship and the immense influence, power, and creativity women have when they are united in friendship, heart, and purpose.

SO LET'S STAY CONNECTED — BECAUSE TOGETHER WE ARE STRONGER.

Visit debbielindell.com to . . .

- Share your story of how this devotional has strengthened your faith!
- Find information about **Designed Sisterhood** events and the **Designed for Life** Women's Conference.
- Be encouraged through *The Pink Mug* podcast: conversations about life, faith, and sisterhood.
- Check out my speaking schedule.
- Discover additional resources, including the *She Believes* book and study guide.

Follow me on Facebook and Instagram
#shepraysbook #shebelievesbook